SO-DZF-622

Computational Practice

Skills Review

PRENTICE HALL
A Division of Simon & Schuster
Needham Heights, Massachusetts 02194
Englewood Cliffs, New Jersey 07632

ISBN: 0-13-839077-0

Printed in the United States of America

3 4 5 6 7 8 9   99 98

Contents

NAME _____ CLASS _____ DATE _____

Reading and Writing Whole Numbers

Reading Whole Numbers

Read 86,200,721

Look at the digits in the place value chart below.

First, read each nonzero period of digits, starting on the left.
Then name the period.

BILLIONS			MILLIONS			THOUSANDS			ONES		
hundred billions	ten billions	billions	hundred millions	ten millions	millions	hundred thousands	ten thousands	thousands	hundreds	tens	ones
				8	6	2	0	0	7	2	1

$$\underline{86,} \qquad\qquad \underline{200,} \qquad\qquad \underline{721}$$
↑ ↑ ↑

eighty-six million, two hundred thousand, seven hundred twenty-one
↑
Do not say *and*.

When a period contains only zeros, do not name it.

$$\underline{5,} \quad 000, \quad \underline{203}$$
↑ ↑

five million, two hundred three
↑
Do not say *thousand*.

Write each number in words.

1. 704 _____

2. 5,038 _____

3. 36,412 _____

4. 300,000 _____

5. 2,000,020 _____

6. 700,321,015 _____

_____

Writing Large Whole Numbers

Writing Whole Numbers

Write in standard form: three million, one hundred two thousand.

The first period is millions.
Write 3 in the millions period.

___ ___ __3__ , ___ ___ ___ , ___ ___ ___

    millions   thousands   ones

The next period is thousands.
Write 102 in the thousands period.

___ ___ __3__ , __1__ __0__ __2__ , ___ ___ ___

    millions   thousands   ones

Remember that each period, except for
the leftmost period, must have three
digits. Insert zeros for any missing
digits. Since there are no digits
for the ones period, write zeros to
complete the number.

___ ___ __3__ , __1__ __0__ __2__ , __0__ __0__ __0__

    millions   thousands   ones

<u>3 million</u> <u>102 thousand</u>
     ↓   ↓
___ ___ __3__ , __1__ __0__ __2__ , __0__ __0__ __0__

For each word name, determine if the number is written correctly.
If the number is correct, write _correct_. If it is not, write the
correct number.

1. Two million, six hundred four thousand   2,604 _____

2. Three million, fifty-six thousand   3,056,000 _____

3. Eight hundred three million, thirty-seven   803,037 _____

4. Nine hundred fifteen billion   915,000,000 _____

Write each number in standard form.

5. Six thousand, thirty-two _____

6. Eight thousand, two _____

7. Seventy-three thousand _____

8. Fifty million, two hundred ninety-one _____

9. Eight million, twenty-five thousand _____

Writing Large Whole Numbers

Write each number in standard form, using commas.

1. eight thousand _____

2. six hundred eighty thousand, five hundred _____

3. one billion _____

4. nine hundred _____

5. two hundred eighty million, five hundred thousand _____

6. six hundred thousand, seven hundred _____

7. one thousand, two hundred _____

8. three thousand, three hundred _____

9. seven hundred four _____

10. fifty thousand _____

11. nine billion, five hundred thousand, seven hundred twenty-one _____

12. four hundred thousand, sixteen _____

13. twenty million, ninety thousand, six _____

14. three hundred million, nine hundred thousand _____

15. fifty thousand, forty-eight _____

16. eight hundred million, six thousand _____

17. seven trillion _____

18. five hundred three _____

19. four thousand eight _____

20. twenty-five thousand, twenty-three _____

Rounding Whole Numbers

Whole Numbers

One of the world's greatest adventure stories was first published in 1719 by the English writer Daniel Defoe. What was the book's title?

To solve:

1. Work each exercise.
2. Find the first digit of each rounded number to the left of the clue box. Find the second digit above the clue box. Find the letter at the intersection of the row and column.
3. Write that letter above the number of the exercise below.

Example: 1. Round 53 to the nearest ten.

Solution: 50   The letter at the intersection of 5 and 0 is *N*. Write *N* above 1.

	0	1	2	3	4
1	E	R	S	A	B
2	E	T	H	C	O
3	S	I	D	M	E
4	O	F	O	S	I
5	N	U	O	N	N
6	O	N	S	R	I
7	S	N	E	O	I
8	R	P	T	E	C

Round each of the following to the place indicated.

Ten: **2.** 41 _____   **3.** 15 _____   **4.** 118 _____

Hundred: **5.** 773 _____   **6.** 4,350 _____   **7.** 6,125 _____

Thousand: **8.** 6,607 _____   **9.** 63,333 _____   **10.** 51,260 _____

Ten thousand: **11.** 236,001 _____   **12.** 842,219 _____

Hundred thousand: **13.** 1,412,611 _____   **14.** 4,160,317 _____

THE LIFE AND STRANGE SURPRISING ADVENTURES OF

__ __ __ __ __ __ __ N   __ __ __ __ __ __
 9 2 13 6 7 4 11 1   12 5 10 8 14 3

NAME _____ CLASS _____ DATE _____

Adding Whole Numbers

Add: 8,742 + 186 + 385

First, estimate the sum.

8,742 → 8,700	Round each addend to the greatest place of the smallest addend.
186 → 200	The smallest addend is 186.
+ 385 → + 400	The greatest place in 186 is hundreds.
9,300	Round all addends to the nearest hundred.
	Add to estimate the sum.

Now add.

```
  8,742
    186
+   385
  9,313
```

To check:

a. Compare the sum with the estimated sum. Is 9,313 close to 9,300? Yes.

b. Add up.
```
  8,742 ↑
    186 |
+   385 |
  9,313
```

Write the estimated sum to the right of each problem. Then add and check.

1. 38
  + 27
_____

2. 56
  + 21
_____

3. 25
   34
  + 87
_____

4. 16
  98
  + 44
_____

5. 348
  + 267
_____

6. 4,529
  + 3,874
_____

7. 623
  415
  + 381
_____

8. 7,356
  4,218
  + 5,033
_____

9. 14,386
  + 27,121
_____

Subtracting Whole Numbers

Subtract: 308 − 57

First, estimate the difference.

Round each number to the greatest place
of the smallest number.
The smallest number is 57.

$308 \rightarrow 310$ The greatest place in 57 is tens.
$\underline{-57 \rightarrow \underline{-60}}$ Round both numbers to the nearest ten.
250 Subtract to estimate the difference.

Now subtract.

$$\begin{array}{r} 308 \\ -57 \\ \hline 1 \end{array}$$ $8 - 7 = 1$

$$\begin{array}{r} \overset{2}{\cancel{3}}\overset{10}{0}8 \\ -57 \\ \hline 51 \end{array}$$ Regroup 3 hundreds as 2 hundreds 10 tens.
$10 - 5 = 5$

$$\begin{array}{r} \overset{2}{\cancel{3}}\overset{10}{0}8 \\ -57 \\ \hline 251 \end{array}$$ $2 - 0 = 2$

To check:

a. Compare the difference with the estimated difference.
Is 251 close to 250? Yes.

b. Add the difference to the number subtracted.
The sum should be the number you subtracted from.

$$\begin{array}{r} 251 \\ +57 \\ \hline 308 \end{array}$$

**Write the estimated difference to the right of each problem. Then
subtract and check.**

1.	2.	3.	4.
$\begin{array}{r} 60 \\ -23 \\ \hline \end{array}$	$\begin{array}{r} 72 \\ -28 \\ \hline \end{array}$	$\begin{array}{r} 40 \\ -16 \\ \hline \end{array}$	$\begin{array}{r} 360 \\ -72 \\ \hline \end{array}$

5.	6.	7.	8.
$\begin{array}{r} 904 \\ -685 \\ \hline \end{array}$	$\begin{array}{r} 700 \\ -519 \\ \hline \end{array}$	$\begin{array}{r} 41,065 \\ -21,887 \\ \hline \end{array}$	$\begin{array}{r} 50,381 \\ -19,872 \\ \hline \end{array}$

NAME _____ CLASS _____ DATE _____

Subtracting Whole Numbers

What is the popular name of Ludwig van Beethoven's Third Symphony?

To solve:

1. Work each exercise, transferring digits as indicated by arrows.
2. Match each number in the row of boxes below with a letter of the alphabet. Write the letter below the box.

Subtract.

1.
```
  4 7
-   5
```

2.
```
  7☐
-   8
```

3.
```
  8☐
- 3 2
```

4.
```
  7
- 5 4
```

5.
```
  8 7
- 8 2
```

6.
```
  ☐ 0
- 1 5
```

7.
```
  ☐☐ 7
- 1 3 4
```

8.
```
  7☐ 4
- 4 3 9
```

9.
```
  7 6 8
- 3 4 8
```

10.
```
  ☐ 0 0
- 1 3 3
```

11.
```
  6☐ 8
- 5 6 9
```

12.
```
    4 4
-   2 6
```

13.
```
  8 , 1 1 9
- 5 , 2 4 4
```

14.
```
  9 , 4 6☐
- 5 , 8 3 8
```

15.
```
  ☐ , ☐ 0 0
- 1 , 5 2 5
```

16.
```
  5 , 0☐ 0
- 2 , 8 6 1
```

17.
```
  3 5 , 8 4 4
- 1 2 , 5 1 3
```

18.
```
  6 4 , 7 1☐
- 3 8 , 9 1 7
```

19.
```
  7 7 , 0 0☐
- 3 8 , 8 5 5
```

20.
```
  8☐ 0 , 2 5☐
- 2 1 6 , 6 3 9
```

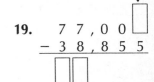

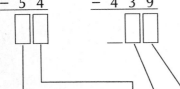

```
A B C D E F G H I  J  K  L  M  N  O  P  Q  R  S  T  U  V  W  X  Y  Z
1 2 3 4 5 6 7 8 9 10 11 12 13 14 15 15 17 18 19 20 21 22 23 24 25 26
```

Multiplying Whole Numbers by One-Digit Numbers

Multiplying With Zeros

Multiply: 280 × 9

First, estimate the product.

280 → 300	Round each factor to its greatest place.
× 9 → × 9	Do not round one-digit factors.
2,700	Multiply to estimate the product.

Now multiply.

```
  280
×   9
2,520 ← 9 × 0 = 0    Don't forget to write 0 in the product.
```

Check your answer.

$9 \times 0 = 0 \rightarrow$ product of the ones place
$9 \times 80 = 720 \rightarrow$ product of the tens place
$9 \times 200 = \underline{1,800} \rightarrow$ product of the hundreds place
$2,520$

Choose the correct product.

1. 700 × 3   **a.** 210   **b.** 2,100   **c.** 2,110   _____

2. 500 × 8   **a.** 4,000   **b.** 400   **c.** 40,000   _____

3. 2 × 600   **a.** 12,000   **b.** 120   **c.** 1,200   _____

4. 3,000 × 9   **a.** 30,000   **b.** 2,700   **c.** 27,000   _____

5. 4,200 × 5   **a.** 20,000   **b.** 21,000   **c.** 2,100   _____

Write the estimated product to the right of each problem. Then multiply and check.

6.   58   **7.**   79   **8.**   155
      ×   4   ×   7   ×   2
      _____   _____   _____

9.   702   **10.**   507   **11.**   620
      ×   3   ×   3   ×   8
      _____   _____   _____

Whole Numbers

NAME _____ CLASS _____ DATE _____

Multiplying Whole Numbers by Numbers Greater Than 10

A Bavarian physicist discovered X-rays accidentally in 1895. Name the physicist.

To solve:

1. Work each exercise.
2. Look at the first two digits of each product. Find the same two digits below.
3. Write the letter of the exercise above the number each time it appears.

Example: Multiply. **E.** 63×13

Solution: 819   Write *E* above 81.

Multiply.

A. $\begin{array}{r} 67 \\ \times 15 \\ \hline \end{array}$	E. $\begin{array}{r} 586 \\ \times 22 \\ \hline \end{array}$	N. $\begin{array}{r} 7,845 \\ \times 35 \\ \hline \end{array}$	L. $\begin{array}{r} 700 \\ \times 41 \\ \hline \end{array}$
D. $\begin{array}{r} 25 \\ \times 34 \\ \hline \end{array}$	L. $\begin{array}{r} 539 \\ \times 63 \\ \hline \end{array}$	E. $\begin{array}{r} 27,554 \\ \times 57 \\ \hline \end{array}$	G. $\begin{array}{r} 23 \\ \times 8,477 \\ \hline \end{array}$
O. $\begin{array}{r} 482 \\ \times 241 \\ \hline \end{array}$	H. $\begin{array}{r} 6,287 \\ \times 853 \\ \hline \end{array}$	R. $\begin{array}{r} 6,543 \\ \times 1,278 \\ \hline \end{array}$	N. $\begin{array}{r} 6,300 \\ \times 92 \\ \hline \end{array}$
I. $\begin{array}{r} 600 \\ \times 900 \\ \hline \end{array}$	N. $\begin{array}{r} 806 \\ \times 255 \\ \hline \end{array}$	M. $\begin{array}{r} 741 \\ \times 605 \\ \hline \end{array}$	C. $\begin{array}{r} 50,809 \\ \times 508 \\ \hline \end{array}$

T. 54×958 _____

W. 791×854 _____

O. Multiply 78 by 29. _____

R. Solve: $98 \times 48 = n$ _____

__ __ __ _E_ __ __   __ __ __ __ __ __
67 54 28 53 81 33 44   25 22 27 83 10 85

__ __ __ __ __ __ __ __
47 11 12 20 51 19 15 57

9

Dividing Whole Numbers by One-Digit Divisors

Zeros in the Quotient

Divide: 1,463 by 7

```
    20
7)1,463     7 is greater than 1. Underline the 4 to help you
  14        remember where to put the first digit in the quotient.
   06       14 ÷ 7 = 2. Write 2 over the underlined 4.
            Multiply 7 by 2. Write 14 below 14 in the dividend.
            Then subtract.
```

Bring down the 6. 7 is greater than 6.
Write a zero above the 6.

```
   209
7)1,463     Bring down the 3.
  1         63 ÷ 7 = 9. Write 9 over the 3 in the dividend.
   063      Multiply 7 by 9. Write 63 below 63 and subtract.
    63      The remainder is zero.
     0
```

Check your answer.

```
   209
×    7
 1,463
```

Choose the correct quotient.

1. 7)420   **a.** 6   **b.** 60   **c.** 16   _____

2. 2)1,012   **a.** 56   **b.** 156   **c.** 506   _____

3. 8)2,448   **a.** 136   **b.** 306   **c.** 36   _____

4. 3)3,240   **a.** 1,080   **b.** 18   **c.** 108   _____

Divide and check.

5. 6)408   6. 3)1,527   7. 4)828   8. 5)20,355

9. 7)39,221   10. 6)1,020   11. 9)7,434   12. 3)1,224

Whole Numbers

NAME _____ CLASS _____ DATE _____

Dividing Whole Numbers by One-Digit Divisors

What American novelist wrote *The Deerslayer*
and *The Last of the Mohicans?*

To solve:

1. Work each exercise.
2. Look at the last two digits of each quotient. Find the same two digits below.
3. Write the letter of the exercise above the number each time it appears.

Example: Divide.   J. 6)426

Solution: 71   Write J above 71.

Divide.

S. 4)48   I. 3)234   R. 8)512

N. 7)854   E. 2)1,390   P. 5)4,165

M. 9)19,305   O. 6)35,418   C. 7)49,203

A. 3)18,078   F. 6)49,512   O. 4)10,024

E. 9)32,175   M. 7)56,861   R. 8)33,504

__J__ ___ ___ ___ ___   ___ ___ ___ ___ ___ ___ ___ ___
71 26 23 75 12   52 95 22 78 45 03 64 75

___ ___ ___ ___ ___ ___
29 03 06 33 95 88

Dividing Whole Numbers by Numbers Greater Than 10

Whole Numbers

Positioning the Quotient

Divide: 23,568 by 58

```
      40
58)23,568
   23 2
      36
```

58 is greater than 2 or 23, so divide 58 into 235. Underline the 5 to help you remember where to put the first digit in the quotient.

Think: 58 rounds to 60, and 235 rounds to 240. Try 4. Write 4 above the underlined 5.

Multiply: 4 × 58 = 232. Subtract.
58 is greater than 3. Bring down the 6.
58 is greater than 36. Write a zero above the 6.

```
      406 R20
58)23,568
   23 2
      368
      348
       20
```

Bring down the 8.
Think: 58 rounds to 60, and 368 rounds to 370.
Write 6 above the 8.
Multiply: 6 × 58 = 348. Subtract.
The remainder is 20.

Check your answer.

```
     406
   ×  58
   3 248
   20 30
   23 548
 +      20←Remember to add the remainder.
   23,568
```

In each dividend, the underlined digit is the one over which you should write the first digit of the quotient. Write _true_ or _false_.

1. 37)4,938 _____

2. 97)86,521 _____

3. 105)368,100 _____

4. 329)31,465 _____

Divide and check.

5. 32)864

6. 95)6,941

7. 67)20,721

8. 58)406,290

9. 38)21,715

10. 81)49,400

NAME _____ CLASS _____ DATE _____

Dividing Whole Numbers by Numbers Greater Than 10

What was the famous tribute to George Washington uttered by General "Light Horse Harry" Lee at Washington's funeral in 1799?

To solve:

1. Work each exercise.
2. In the clue box find the word that matches each quotient.
3. Write the word above the number of the exercise each time it appears below.

Example: Divide. **1.** $13\overline{)416}$

Solution: 32 The word *of* matches 32. Write *of* above 1.

Divide.

2. $21\overline{)1,743}$	**3.** $83\overline{)1,577}$
4. $67\overline{)8,576}$	**5.** $75\overline{)16,050}$
6. $57\overline{)75,297}$	**7.** $88\overline{)212,608}$
8. $317\overline{)951}$	**9.** $476\overline{)8,568}$
10. $233\overline{)108,345}$	**11.** $304\overline{)245,024}$

Clue Box	
3	first
6	woman
8	family
13	child
18	peace
19	in
32	of
83	and
85	now
87	an
128	the
214	his
230	never
232	victory
234	defeat
251	patriots
287	soldiers
462	minds
465	hearts
801	citizens
806	countrymen
808	elephants
1,321	first
2,416	war
2,511	death
2,614	life

" _____ _____ _____, _____ _____
   6   3   7   8   3

_____, _____ _____ _____ _____
  9   2   6   3   4

_____ OF _____ _____ ."
  10   1   5   11

Factors: Greatest Common Factor (GCF)

Whole Numbers

Finding all the Factors

Name all the factors of 48.

$\dfrac{48}{1)\overline{48}}$ Try every possible factor.
Divide 48 by 1. 1 divides evenly into 48.
Both 1 and 48 are factors of 48.

$\dfrac{24}{2)\overline{48}}$ 2 divides evenly into 48.
Both 2 and 24 are factors of 48.

$\dfrac{16}{3)\overline{48}}$ 3 divides evenly into 48.
Both 3 and 16 are factors of 48.

$\dfrac{12}{4)\overline{48}}$ 4 divides evenly into 48.
Both 4 and 12 are factors of 48.

$\dfrac{9 \text{ R3}}{5)\overline{48}}$ 5 does not divide evenly into 48.
5 is not a factor of 48.

$\dfrac{8}{6)\overline{48}}$ 6 divides evenly into 48.
Both 6 and 8 are factors of 48.

$\dfrac{6 \text{ R6}}{7)\overline{48}}$ 7 does not divide evenly into 48.
7 is not a factor of 48.

$\dfrac{6}{8)\overline{48}}$ 8 divides evenly into 48.
But 6 and 8 are repeat factors.

When factors begin to repeat, stop.
You have found all the factors.
Then list all the factors.
1, 2, 3, 4, 6, 8, 12, 16, 24, 48

Name all the factors of each number. Then name the common factors of each pair of numbers.

1. 16: _____

    24: _____

    16 and 24: _____

2. 81: _____

    99: _____

    81 and 99: _____

Name the greatest common factor of each group of numbers.

3. 16, 38: _____

4. 75, 125: _____

5. 15, 21, 84: _____

6. 72, 144, 360: _____

Factors: Greatest Common Factor (GCF)

The oldest plants on earth are more than 4,000 years old.
What are they and where are they found?

To solve:

1. Work each exercise.
2. Find the first digit of each answer to the left of the clue box. Find the second digit above the clue box. (If an answer has only one digit, place a zero in front of it.) Find the letter at the intersection of the row and column.
3. Write that letter above the number of the exercise each time it appears below.

	0	1	2	3	4	5	6
0	K	A	E	R	S	I	T
1	O	V	N	F	C	B	L
2	P	M	D	W	H	G	U

Example: 1. Name the greatest common factor of 6 and 12.

Solution: 6   The letter at the intersection of 0 and 6 is *T*. Write *T* above 1.

Name the second factor of a pair of factors.

2. 17 is one factor of 34 _____

3. 4 is one factor of 60 _____

4. 23 is one factor of 69 _____

5. 19 is one factor of 95 _____

6. 7 is one factor of 28 _____

7. 3 is one factor of 48 _____

Name the greatest common factor of each pair of numbers.

8. 14 and 28 _____

9. 70 and 120 _____

10. 60 and 84 _____

Name the greatest common factor of each group of numbers.

11. 40, 80, 100 _____

12. 39, 52, 91 _____

13. 21,22, 23 _____

```
__  __  __  __  T  __  __  __  __  __  __     __  __  __  __
3   4   5   6   1  7   2   8   9   10  2      11  5   10  2
```

```
T  __  __  __     __  __     __  __  __  __  __  __  __  __  __  __
1  4   2   2      9   12     8   13  7   5   12  9   4   10  5   13
```

Multiples

Finding the Least Common Multiple

Find the LCM of 8 and 12.
LCM means the least nonzero common multiple.

First, list several multiples of each number.

Multiples of 8	Multiples of 12
$0 \times 8 = 0$	$0 \times 12 = 0$
$1 \times 8 = 8$	$1 \times 12 = 12$
$2 \times 8 = 16$	$2 \times 12 = 24$
$3 \times 8 = 24$	$3 \times 12 = 36$
$4 \times 8 = 32$	$4 \times 12 = 48$
$5 \times 8 = 40$	$5 \times 12 = 60$
$6 \times 8 = 48$	$6 \times 12 = 72$

The least nonzero common multiple (LCM) is 24.

Remember that the LCM of a pair of numbers could be the
larger of the two numbers.
For example, the LCM of 6 and 12 is 12, since 12 is a multiple
of 6 (6×2).

Choose a multiple for each number.

1. 3   **a.** 16   **b.** 24   **c.** 28 _____

2. 8   **a.** 26   **b.** 32   **c.** 42 _____

3. 12   **a.** 60   **b.** 45   **c.** 30 _____

**Write the first six multiples of each number. Then write the LCM
for each pair.**

4. 12: _____

    15: _____ LCM = _____

5. 9: _____

    6: _____ LCM = _____

Find the LCM of each set of numbers.

6. 9 and 4 _____   **7.** 9 and 15 _____

8. 7 and 9 _____   **9.** 2, 3, and 5 _____

NAME _____ CLASS _____ DATE _____

Multiples

Circle the number that is a multiple of the first number.

1. 3   32   42   52   **2.** 4   85   87   88

3. 8   104 125 133   **4.** 14   112 143 150

5. 15   185 225 215   **6.** 7   36   51   63

Write the first four multiples of each number.

7. 6 _____   **8.** 8 _____

9. 24 _____   **10.** 7 _____

11. 9 _____   **12.** 13 _____

Write the first three nonzero common multiples of each pair.

13. 2 and 5 _____   **14.** 2 and 7 _____

15. 8 and 3 _____   **16.** 8 and 6 _____

17. 3 and 7 _____   **18.** 4 and 5 _____

Write the least common multiple of each group.

19. 3 and 5 _____   **20.** 25 and 75 _____   **21.** 3, 4, and 5 _____

22. 5 and 6 _____   **23.** 5, 15, and 20 _____   **24.** 6, 8, and 12 _____

25. 3 and 8 _____   **26.** 6 and 32 _____   **27.** 2, 6, and 24 _____

28. 2 and 7 _____   **29.** 9 and 17 _____   **30.** 4, 5, and 7 _____

Estimation/Mental Math

Whole Numbers

Do these exercises mentally.

1. Which names the greatest number? _____

   $36 \div 4$ 36×4 $36 - 4$ $36 + 4$

2. Which names the least number? _____

   $24 + 4$ $24 - 4$ $24 \div 4$ 24×4

3. 30 is 25 less than what number? _____

4. Find the sum of $82 + 6$. Then subtract 8. _____

5. Don filled 47 boxes. Ted filled 14 more than Don.

   How many boxes did Ted fill? _____

6. After John had sold 42 papers, he had 18 papers left.

   How many papers did he have? _____

7. The sum of 16 and a number is 30. What is the number? _____

8. Which is equal to 210×399: 8,379, 83,790, or 837,900? _____

9. Round each addend to the nearest hundred and add. $482 + 239$ _____

10. Of 184 parking places, only 74 were filled.

    How many places were not filled? _____

11. Find the sum by adding and subtracting:

    $6,365 + 2,980 = (6,365 + 3,000) -$ _____ $=$ _____

12. Find the difference by subtracting and adding:

    $7,463 - 3,972 = (7,463 - 4,000) +$ _____ $=$ _____

13. Estimate the sum: $263,000 + 379,010$ _____

14. Estimate the difference: $693,942 - 317,000$ _____

15. Round each number and multiply. $752 \times 4,380$ _____

16. Round the dividend so that it can be divided exactly by the divisor. $73,152 \div 38$

    _____

NAME _____ CLASS _____ DATE _____

Mixed Review

Write in words.

1. 20,497 _____

2. 687,502,000 _____

_____

3. 3,460,005 _____

Write the standard form using commas.

4. Thirty-two billion, six hundred eighteen million, nine thousand, twelve _____

5. Four hundred forty-three million, seventy-five thousand _____

Round to the place indicated.

6. 742 to the nearest ten _____

7. 586,598 to the nearest thousand _____

8. 8,397,641 to the nearest ten thousand _____

Add.

9.   26,591
    32,788
  + 10,456

10. 348 + 670 + 496 + 285 _____

11. 5,674 + 62 + 817 + 39 _____

Subtract.

12.   71,632
   − 48,755

13. 300,000 − 176,278 _____

14. Take 26,593 from 50,218. _____

Multiply.

15. 285 × 697 _____

16.   3,657
   ×   4

17.   893
   × 56

Divide.

18. $8)\overline{3,672}$

19. $28)\overline{10,192}$

20. List all the factors of 50. _____

21. Name the greatest common factor of 36 and 54. _____

Reading Decimals

Decimal Place Values

Read 138.7693.

Use the place value chart at the right to help name place values.

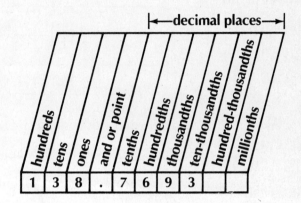

Read the whole number.
Say *and* for the decimal point.
Read the remaining digits the same way you read whole numbers.
Then name the place value of the last digit.
3 is in the ten-thousandths place.

$$\underline{138} \qquad . \qquad \underline{7693}$$

↑   ↑   ↑

one hundred thirty-eight and seven thousand, six hundred ninety-three ten-thousandths

↑

Do not say *and* here.

In each number, name the place value of the last digit.

1. 3.7962 _____ **2.** 0.08135 _____

3. 21.385 _____ **4.** 0.612547 _____

Write the word name for each number.

5. 8.3 _____

6. 1.7 _____

7. 0.09 _____

8. 37.54 _____

9. 216.007 _____

10. 13.621 _____

11. 1.5291 _____

_____

12. 4.02056 _____

Decimals

Reading Decimals

Write in words.

1. 0.5 _____

2. 0.003 _____

3. 3.087 _____

4. 0.49 _____

5. 0.00007 _____

6. 0.75 _____

7. 0.06 _____

8. 8.37 _____

9. 0.00004 _____

10. 3.5 _____

11. 0.000002 _____

12. 0.08 _____

13. 2.8 _____

14. 0.0051 _____

15. 0.0001 _____

16. 35 _____

17. 17.028 _____

18. 0.0006 _____

19. 0.396 _____

20. 0.015 _____

21. 1.604 _____

22. 5.48 _____

Writing Decimals

Decimal Point Placement

Write three and sixty-four thousandths in standard form.

Use the simplified place value chart at the right to help place the digits.
Write a decimal point for *and*.
Write 3 before *and*.
Thousandths means three decimal places. Write 4 in the thousandths place and 6 before the 4.
Write a zero after the decimal point to fill the tenths place.

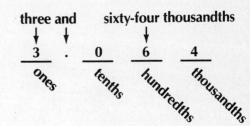

For each given word name, determine if the number is written correctly. If the number is correct, write *correct*. If it is not, write the correct number.

1. Three hundred fifty-five thousandths   300.055 _____

2. Eighty-six and four hundredths   86.04 _____

3. Twenty-two ten-thousandths   0.022 _____

4. Eight hundred and fifteen hundredths   800.15 _____

5. One and seven hundred-thousandths   1.0007 _____

Write each number in standard form.

6. Seventeen and five tenths _____

7. Three hundred four thousandths _____

8. Six hundred and eighty-five thousandths _____

9. One hundred five ten-thousandths _____

10. Four hundred ten and one thousand five ten-thousandths _____

11. Eighty-six hundred-thousandths _____

12. Five hundred twenty-six millionths _____

Decimals

Rounding Decimals

Rounding to the Correct Place

Round 0.6953 to the nearest hundredth.

The place value chart at the right will help you find the place to be rounded.

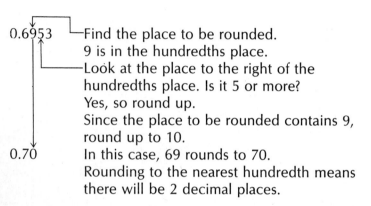

0	.	6	9	5	3
ones		tenths	hundredths	thousandths	ten-thousandths

0.6953 — Find the place to be rounded.
9 is in the hundredths place.
— Look at the place to the right of the hundredths place. Is it 5 or more? Yes, so round up.
Since the place to be rounded contains 9, round up to 10.
0.70   In this case, 69 rounds to 70.
Rounding to the nearest hundredth means there will be 2 decimal places.

Choose the correct answer.

1. Round 2.8615 to the nearest hundredth.
    a. 2.87   **b.** 2.9   **c.** 2.86   **d.** 2.862   _____

2. Round 0.83979 to the nearest thousandth.
    a. 0.840   **b.** 0.84   **c.** 0.8398   **d.** 0.839   _____

3. Round $76.5065 to the nearest cent.
    a. $76.5   **b.** $76.505   **c.** $76.50   **d.** $76.51   _____

Round each number to the nearest hundredth.

4. 24.896 _____

5. 0.08345 _____

6. 265.9952 _____

Round each number to the nearest ten-thousandth.

7. 0.085423 _____

8. 2.845074 _____

9. 0.347952 _____

Decimals

Rounding Decimals

Using Rounded Numbers for Estimates

You can estimate calculations with decimals by rounding the decimals to the nearest whole number. By using a different method of estimating, you can obtain a range within which the precise calculation falls.

Locate a decimal between two consecutive whole numbers. The first whole number is the number to the left of the decimal point. The second number is 1 more. For example, 3.77 is between 3 and 3 + 1, or 4.

Example: Find the range for the total cost of the following: $3.77, $1.98, $2.35, $.48, and $1.45.

Solution: Locate each decimal between two consecutive whole numbers. Then add the whole numbers.

	$3.77 is between $3 and $4
1.98	1 2
2.35	2 3
.48	0 1
1.45	+ 1 + 2
	$7 $12

The total cost for the items is between $7 and $12.

Estimate the sum in two ways. First, round each decimal to the nearest whole number and add. Then estimate by finding the range.

1. 21.8 + 86.92 + 113.2 + 9.886 _____

2. 113.6 + 49.1 + 3.4 + 677.51 _____

3. 208.3 + 9.2 + 18.7 + 102.05 _____

4. 72.008 + 19.4 + 21.4 + 45.4 _____

Find each range to determine whether $20 is enough money to pay for items with the given prices.

5. $13.98, $2.45, $1.86 _____

6. $3.45, $9.98, $3.95, $1.98 _____

Solve.

*7. About how much change would you expect to have from a $20-bill if you bought items with the following prices: $.35, $1.98, $5.50, $8.20, and $.50. Estimate your answer both ways. Which method is more useful in this case?

Decimals

Comparing Decimals

Comparing Correct Places

Which is greater: 0.86 or 0.091?

To compare two decimal numbers, both must have the same number of digits after the decimal point.

$0.86 \rightarrow 0.860$ Write zeros until the decimals
$0.091 \rightarrow 0.091$ have the same number of places.

Now compare the decimals digit by digit.

0.860
↓
0.091

$8 > 0$, so $0.860 > 0.091$

Which is greater?

1. 17.9 or 17.953 _____

2. 0.8 or 0.183 _____

3. 24.8 or 31.72 _____

4. 0.505 or 0.55 _____

Which is less?

5. 0.06 or 0.006 _____

6. 3.98 or 20.099 _____

7. 0.23 or 0.088 _____

8. 0.02019 or 0.020019 _____

Write in order from greatest to least.

9. 0.23, 0.320, 0.023, 2.3, 2.03 _____

10. 0.42, 1.4, 0.308, 34 _____

11. 2.9, 0.88, 0.9203, 1.802 _____

Write in order from least to greatest.

12. 0.98, 0.918, 0.098, 1.98 _____

13. 2.09, 2.19, 2.18, 2.9 _____

14. 23.87, 412.802, 311.88, 84.399, 9.98 _____

Decimals

Adding Decimals

Decimal Point Placement

Add: 3.6 + 12.51 + 21

First, estimate the sum.
Round each addend to the greatest
place of the smallest addend.
The smallest addend is 3.6.
The greatest place in 3.6 is ones.

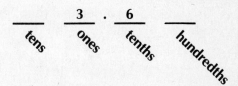

$$3.6 \rightarrow \quad 4$$
$$12.51 \rightarrow \quad 13$$
$$\underline{+\ 21\ \rightarrow\underline{+\ 21}}$$
$$\qquad\qquad 38$$

Round all addends to the nearest whole number.

Add to estimate the sum.

Now add.

┌─────── Line up the decimal points.
↓
3.60   Write ending zeros so that all addends will
12.51   have the same number of places.
+ 21.00
───────
37.11

Check your answer by adding up.

3.60 ↑
12.51
+ 21.00
───────
37.11

Compare the sum to the estimated sum. Is 37.11 close to 38?
Yes.

Choose the correct sum.

1. 2 + 3.82 + 11.6   **a.** 69.8   **b.** 17.42   **c.** 15.62   _____

2. 12.6 + 5.83 + 7   **a.** 25.43   **b.** 78.43   **c.** 19.13   _____

3. 42.194 + 8 + 3.85   **a.** 54.044   **b.** 46.844   **c.** 46.124   _____

Add and check.

4. 34 + 0.67 + 12.71 _____   **5.** 326.13 + 413 + 882.6 _____

6. 138.96 + 244 + 3.8 _____   **7.** 4.22 + 9.109 + 0.7 _____

Decimals (side tab)

Adding Decimals

What painting by Pablo Picasso was inspired by the 1937 bombing of a village in northern Spain?

To solve:

1. Work each exercise, transferring digits as indicated by arrows.
2. Match each number in the row of boxes below with a letter of the alphabet. Write the letter below the box.

Add.

1.
```
    0 . 6
    0 . 2
  + 0 . 1
  _____
   __ . □
```

2.
```
    0 . □
    0 . 8
  + 0 . 4
  _____
   __ . □
```

3.
```
   □ . 3
   2 . 1
   4 . 2
 + 0 . 3
 _____
   □ . __
```

4.
```
    0 . 0 6
    0 . 0 7
  + 0 . 0 4
  _____
   __ . □
```

5.
```
    0 . 3 □
    4 . 2 8
  + 3 . 1 5
  _____
   __ . □ □
```

6.
```
    9 . □ □
    2 . 0 7
    9 . 3
  + 0 . 0 8
  _____
   □ □ . □
```

7.
```
    6 . 2 5
    8 . 9 1
  +   4 . 3 6
  _____
   □ . __ __
```

8.
```
    □ . 8 2
    5 . 7
  + 6 . 3 6
  _____
   □ . □ □
```

9.
```
    □ . □ 4 3
    8 . 7 5 2
    7 . 3 1 8
  +   0 . 6 0 1
  _____
   □ □ . □ □
```

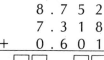

10.
```
    4 2 . 7 7
    3 8 . 1 9
  +   5 7 . 0 9
  _____
   □ □ . __ __
```

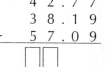

11.
```
    5 5 . □ □
    1 0 9 . 6
  +       3 . 0 7
  _____
   □ □ . __ □
```

10.
```
    □ . □ 6
    0 . 0 9
    8 3 . 1 6 8
  +   0 . 5 4 3
  _____
   □ □ . □ □ □
```

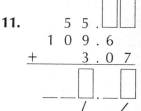

```
□ □ □ □ □ □ □ □ □ □ □ □
```

___ ___ ___ ___ ___ ___ ___ ___ ___ ___ ___ ___

```
A B C D E F G H I J K L M N O P Q R S T U V W X Y Z
1 2 3 4 5 6 7 8 9 10 11 12 13 14 15 16 17 18 19 20 21 22 23 24 25 26
```

Decimals

Subtracting Decimals

Subtract: 12.053 − 3.714

First, estimate the difference.

12.053→ 12   Round both numbers to the nearest whole number.
− 3.714→− 4
                8   Subtract to estimate the difference.

Now subtract. Use a place value chart to help with regrouping.

tens	ones	.	tenths	hundredths	thousandths
				④	⑬
1	2	.	0	5̶	3̶
−	3	.	7	1	4
				3	9

Regroup 5 hundredths
as 4 hundredths 10 thousandths.
Subtract the thousandths.
Subtract the hundredths.

tens	ones	.	tenths	hundredths	thousandths
⓪	⑪	.	⑩	④	⑬
1̶	2̶	.	0̶	5̶	3̶
−	3	.	7	1	4
	8	.	3	3	9

Regroup 2 ones
as 1 one 10 tenths.
Subtract the tenths.
Remember to place the decimal point.
Regroup 1 ten as 10 ones.
Subtract the ones.

Choose the correct difference.

1. 5.03 − 0.28   a. 4.85   b. 4.75   c. 5.75   _____

2. 6 − 3.812   a. 2.188   b. 3.188   c. 2.298   _____

3. 20.6 − 5.772   a. 15.828   b. 14.828   c. 14.938   _____

4. 55 − 19.309   a. 36.691   b. 35.701   c. 35.691   _____

First estimate the difference. Then subtract and check.

5.   4.07   6.   7.00   7.   12.023   8.   23.107
   − 2.18   − 4.35   − 5.158   − 8.532
   _____   _____   _____   _____

9.   105   10.   219.04   11. $800   12. $25
   − 83.612   − 188.753   − 471.16   − 17.08
   _____   _____   _____   _____

Multiplying Decimals

Decimal Point Placement

Multiply: 0.34 × 0.12

First, estimate the product.

0.34→   0.3   Round each factor to its greatest place.
0.12→× 0.1   Then multiply to get an estimate.
        0.03   Write an extra zero to the left of the
                     numbers to make 2 decimal places.

Now multiply.

```
   0.34     2 decimal places     Check:     0.12
 × 0.12     2 decimal places              × 0.34     Reverse the factors.
   68                                        48
   34                                        36
 0.0408     4 decimal places              0.0408
```
↑
└Write an extra zero
  to the left of the numbers
  to make 4 decimal places.

Place the decimal point in each product. Write zeros as necessary.

1.	**2.**	**3.**	**4.**
3.4	0.43	1.03	0.25
× 0.02	× 0.006	× 0.04	× 0.46
68	258	412	1150

Choose the best estimate.

5. 2.6 × 1.8   **a.** 3   **b.** 6   **c.** 4   _____

6. 7.3 × 0.03   **a.** 21   **b.** 2.1   **c.** 0.21   _____

7. 1.34 × 0.15   **a.** 0.2   **b.** 2   **c.** 1.5   _____

8. 0.6 × 0.5   **a.** 0.03   **b.** 0.3   **c.** 3.00   _____

First, estimate each product. Then multiply and check.

9.	**10.**
0.03	0.105
× 2	× 0.7
_____	_____

11.	**12.**
16	7.19
× 0.008	× 0.256
_____	_____

Multiplying Decimals

Multiply.

1. $\begin{array}{r} 0.4 \\ \times\ \ 7 \\ \hline \end{array}$

2. $\begin{array}{r} 54 \\ \times\ 0.72 \\ \hline \end{array}$

3. $\begin{array}{r} 0.651 \\ \times\ \ \ 46 \\ \hline \end{array}$

4. $\begin{array}{r} 0.8242 \\ \times\ \ \ \ \ 9 \\ \hline \end{array}$

5. $\begin{array}{r} 0.85 \\ \times\ \ 30 \\ \hline \end{array}$

6. $\begin{array}{r} 0.07 \\ \times\ \ 16 \\ \hline \end{array}$

7. $\begin{array}{r} 6 \\ \times\ 0.08 \\ \hline \end{array}$

8. $\begin{array}{r} 0.007 \\ \times\ \ \ 13 \\ \hline \end{array}$

9. $\begin{array}{r} 0.0024 \\ \times\ \ \ \ \ 4 \\ \hline \end{array}$

10. $\begin{array}{r} 270 \\ \times\ 3.8 \\ \hline \end{array}$

11. $\begin{array}{r} 0.5 \\ \times\ 0.8 \\ \hline \end{array}$

12. $\begin{array}{r} 0.3 \\ \times\ 0.1 \\ \hline \end{array}$

13. $\begin{array}{r} 0.27 \\ \times\ \ 0.8 \\ \hline \end{array}$

14. $\begin{array}{r} 0.14 \\ \times\ \ 0.4 \\ \hline \end{array}$

15. $\begin{array}{r} 3.2 \\ \times\ 0.35 \\ \hline \end{array}$

16. $\begin{array}{r} 0.08 \\ \times\ 0.52 \\ \hline \end{array}$

17. $\begin{array}{r} 0.245 \\ \times\ \ \ 2.4 \\ \hline \end{array}$

18. $\begin{array}{r} 0.00125 \\ \times\ 0.0144 \\ \hline \end{array}$

19. $\begin{array}{r} 6.15 \\ \times\ 0.004 \\ \hline \end{array}$

20. $\begin{array}{r} 5.219 \\ \times\ 6.32 \\ \hline \end{array}$

21. $\begin{array}{r} 0.0006 \\ \times\ \ \ 0.03 \\ \hline \end{array}$

22. $\begin{array}{r} \$.62 \\ \times\ \ 14 \\ \hline \end{array}$

23. $\begin{array}{r} \$3.77 \\ \times\ \ \ 21 \\ \hline \end{array}$

24. $\begin{array}{r} \$32.10 \\ \times\ \ 0.24 \\ \hline \end{array}$

25. 8×0.6 _____

26. 0.5×0.45 _____

27. Find 0.6 of 42.5. _____

28. Circle the nearest given estimate for $0.48 \times \$15.90$.
   a. $8   **b.** $16   **c.** $25

29. Solve: $0.07 \times 0.3 = n$ _____

Multiplying by Powers of Ten

Manipulating Decimals

Multiply 4.5 by 10; by 100; by 1,000.

$4.5 \times 10 = 45$ There is 1 zero in 10.
Move the decimal point 1 place to the right.

$4.50 \times 100 = 450$ There are 2 zeros in 100.
Move the decimal point 2 places to the right.

$4.500 \times 1,000 = 4,500$ There are 3 zeros in 1,000.
Move the decimal point 3 places to the right.

Multiply 0.72 by 10; by 100; by 1,000.

$0.72 \times 10 = 7.2$ Move the decimal point 1 place to the right.

$0.72 \times 100 = 72$ Move the decimal point 2 places to the right.

$0.720 \times 1,000 = 720$ Move the decimal point 3 places to the right.

Multiply each number by 10.

1. 26 _____ **2.** 20 _____ **3.** 0.2 _____ **4.** 7.8 _____

5. 0.36 _____ **6.** 0.05 _____ **7.** 0.0062 _____ **8.** 538.711 _____

Multiply each number by 100.

9. 38 _____ **10.** 170 _____ **11.** 0.5 _____ **12.** 9.6_____

13. 0.48_____ **14.** 0.0091 _____ **15.** 0.03 _____ **16.** 286.114 _____

Multiply each number by 1,000.

17. 45 _____ **18.** 400 _____ **19.** 0.5 _____ **20.** 12.4 _____

21. 0.78 _____ **22.** 0.0071 _____ **23.** 0.091 _____ **24.** 1,428.092 _____

Multiply each number by 1,000,000.

25. 0.254 _____ **26.** 3.8 _____ **27.** 45.2 _____

28. 0.80463 _____ **29.** 0.000047 _____ **30.** 6.9031 _____

Decimals

Dividing Decimals by Whole Numbers

Divide: 0.15 ÷ 12

First, estimate the quotient.

0.15→0.12   Round the dividend to the nearest
0.12 ÷ 12 = 0.01   multiple of the divisor.
                   Divide to get an estimate.

Now divide.

```
    0.01
12)0.15      Write the decimal point directly above the decimal
    0        point in the dividend.
   15        Write a zero next to the decimal point because 1
   12        cannot be divided by 12.
    3        Divide 15 by 12.
```

```
    0.0125
12)0.1500    Write 2 zeros in the dividend
    0        to complete the division.
   15
   12
   30
   24
   60
   60
    0
```

Check: 0.0125
        ×   12
            250
            125
         0.1500

Place the decimal point in each quotient. Write zeros as necessary.

1. 6)0.33 $\overline{55}$

2. 13)3.25 $\overline{25}$

3. 8)0.288 $\overline{36}$

4. 12)1.656 $\overline{138}$

5. 24)141.36 $\overline{5\ 89}$

6. 58)783.0 $\overline{13\ 5}$

7. 31)1.3268 $\overline{428}$

8. 14)1.05 $\overline{75}$

First, estimate each quotient. Then divide and check.

9. _____ 36)7.2

10. _____ 44)27.94

11. _____ 19)129.2

12. _____ 40)20

13. _____ 500)10

14. _____ 6)38.16

Dividing Decimals by Decimals

Decimal Point Placement

Divide: 0.00798 ÷ 0.21

First, estimate the quotient.

0.21→0.2	Round the divisor to its highest place.
0.00798→0.008	Round the dividend to a number divisible by the divisor.
0.008 ÷ 0.2 = 0.04	Divide to get an estimate.

Now divide.

$0.21\overline{)0.00.798}$

To make the divisor a whole number, move the decimal point two places to the right.
Also move the decimal point 2 places to the right in the dividend.
Write a decimal point in the quotient directly above the decimal point in the dividend.

```
        0.038        ⌐Write a zero since 7        Check:    0.038        Use the original
0.21)0.00.798         cannot be divided by 21.            ×  0.21        divisor.
        0                                                      38
       79                                                      76
       63                                                   0.00798
      168
      168
        0
```

Choose the problem that is equivalent to the given problem.

1. $3.2\overline{)16}$	**a.** $32\overline{)16.0}$	**b.** $32\overline{)160}$	**c.** $32\overline{)1600}$ _____
2. $0.08\overline{)7}$	**a.** $8\overline{)7000}$	**b.** $8\overline{)70}$	**c.** $8\overline{)700}$ _____
3. $0.2\overline{)34}$	**a.** $2\overline{)3.4}$	**b.** $2\overline{)34}$	**c.** $2\overline{)340}$ _____
4. $5.81\overline{)0.436}$	**a.** $581\overline{)43.6}$	**b.** $581\overline{)4.36}$	**c.** $581\overline{)436}$ _____

Place the decimal point in each quotient. You will need to write zeros in the quotient to make the correct number of places.

5. $0.8\overline{)0.024}^{\;3}$	**6.** $1.7\overline{)0.0187}^{\;11}$	**7.** $0.25\overline{)0.015}^{\;6}$	**8.** $0.804\overline{)0.001608}^{\;2}$

Dividing Decimals by Decimals

In 1963, a Russian became the first woman to travel in space, orbiting the earth 48 times. What was her name?

To solve:

1. Work each exercise.
2. Find each answer below.
3. Write the letter of the exercise above the answer each time it appears.

Example: Divide.   E. $0.3)\overline{12.6}$

Solution: 42   Write *E* above 42.

Divide.

T. $0.4)\overline{0.3112}$

A. $0.4)\overline{12}$

H. $0.4)\overline{190.8}$

O. $0.6)\overline{304.284}$

I. $0.8)\overline{0.0288}$

S. $6.8)\overline{153.00}$

L. $0.3)\overline{81}$

R. $0.07)\overline{26.67}$

N. $0.74)\overline{4.6028}$

V. $0.05)\overline{0.00085}$

A. $4.45)\overline{355.11}$

A. $0.32)\overline{24}$

K. $0.006)\overline{0.738}$

N. $0.825)\overline{0.37125}$

V. $5.246)\overline{35.6728}$

___	___	___	E	___	___	___	___	___
6.8	30	270	42	6.22	0.778	0.036	0.45	79.8

___	E	___	E	___	___	___	___	___
0.778	42	381	42	22.5	477	123	507.14	0.017	75

Decimals

Dividing by Powers of Ten

Decimal Point Placement

Divide 8.6 by 10; by 100; by 1,000.

8.6 ÷ 10 = 0.86
There is 1 zero in 10.
Move the decimal point 1 place to the left.

08.6 ÷ 100 = 0.086
There are 2 zeros in 100.
Move the decimal point 2 places to the left.

008.6 ÷ 1,000 = 0.0086
There are 3 zeros in 1,000.
Move the decimal point 3 places to the left.

Divide 0.37 by 10; by 100; by 1,000.

0.37 ÷ 10 = 0.037
Move the decimal point 1 place to the left.

00.37 ÷ 100 = 0.0037
Move the decimal point 2 places to the left.

000.37 ÷ 1,000 = 0.00037
Move the decimal point 3 places to the left.

Choose the correct quotient.

1. 0.680 ÷ 10   a. 6.8   b. 0.068   c. 0.0068   _____

2. 3.5 ÷ 100   a. 0.0035   b. 0.035   c. 0.35   _____

3. 0.6 ÷ 1000   a. 0.0006   b. 0.06   c. 0.006   _____

Divide each number by 10.

4. 45 _____   5. 312.3 _____   6. 0.9 _____   7. 0.03 _____

8. 702 _____   9. 0.475 _____   10. 8.67 _____   11. 1.8 _____

Divide each number by 100.

12. 45 _____   13. 383.2 _____   14. 0.08 _____   15. 0.328 _____

16. 60.2 _____   17. 1.835 _____   18. 597.06 _____   19. 0.9573 _____

Divide each number by 1,000.

20. 350 _____   21. 4,500 _____   22. 6.8 _____

23. 0.921 _____

24. Divide 23,000,000 by 1,000,000,000. _____

Estimation/Mental Math

Estimate to the nearest whole number.

1. 35.28 + 7.926 + 15.099 + 8.52 _____
2. 19.523 − 11.09 _____

3. 3.62 + 1.43 + 4.009 + 5.64 _____
4. 6.078 − 2.7439 _____

Estimate to the nearest tenth.

5. 7.406 + 9.219 + 11.098 + 2.354 _____
6. 8.52 − 3.07 _____

7. 0.15621 + 0.142 + 0.7163 + 1.23 _____
8. 0.309 − 0.192 _____

Estimate by rounding each number to its greatest place value position.

9. 10.8 × 6.03 _____
10. 9.72 ÷ 2.4 _____

11. 3.156 × 4.78 _____
12. 7.808 ÷ 16 _____

13. 3.06 × 7.994 _____
14. 68.5 ÷ 7.2 _____

15. 7.02 × 1.363 _____
16. 15.93 ÷ 5.3 _____

Divide by 10.

17. 40 _____ **18.** 50 _____ **19.** 72 _____ **20.** 68 _____ **21.** 540 _____

Multiply by 100.

22. 4 _____ **23.** 50 _____ **24.** 400 _____ **25.** 65 _____ **26.** 650 _____

Divide by 100.

27. 860 _____ **28.** 8,600 _____ **29.** 86,000 _____ **30.** 860,000 _____

Divide by 50.

31. 100 _____ **32.** 1,000 _____ **33.** 200 _____ **34.** 2,000 _____

Solve mentally.

35. Mr. Franca bought a shirt for $12.95, slacks for $25.49, a coat for $62.75, and a tie for $10.35.

    a. Estimate the total cost to the nearest ten dollars. _____

    b. Estimate Mr. Franca's change from $120. _____

36. Adam withdrew $300 from his account of $792. How much money did he

    have left? _____

37. Elena bought 10 hamburgers at $.49 each. Was $5.00 enough to pay for them? _____

Calculator

When you compare decimals, subtract the second number from
the first number. If the answer is positive, the first number is
greater than the second. If the result is negative, the first number
is less than the second. If the result is 0, the numbers are equal.

Compare these decimals. Use >, <, or =.

1. 0.835 ____ 0.8367   **2.** 2.167 ____ 2.167

3. 3.4861 ____ 3.4661   **4.** 0.0025 ____ 0.025

5. 3.0411 ____ 3.141   **6.** 3.882 ____ 3.8982

7. 0.567 ____ 2.567   **8.** 1.3123 ____ 1.3113

9. 26.0106 ____ 26.1006   **10.** 8.242 ____ 8.422

11. 30.5 ____ 30.500   **12.** 0.6219 ____ 0.6129

13. 0.8679 ____ 0.8769   **14.** 1.854 ____ 2.854

15. 5.12 ____ 5.123   **16.** 0.007 ____ 0.0007

Multiply.

17. 52 × 0.04 _____   **18.** 0.0038 × 0.13 _____

19. 86 × 0.225 _____   **20.** 0.016 × 0.016 _____

21. 16 × 0.85 _____   **22.** 0.666 × 1.5 _____

23. 850 × 0.2 _____   **24.** 363 × 1.3 _____

25. 2.4 × 0.07 _____   **26.** 0.18 × 1.26 _____

27. 9.3 × 0.105 _____   **28.** 6 × 0.852 _____

29. 247 × 0.5 _____   **30.** 2.78 × 0.319 _____

Divide.

31. 7,113.75 ÷ 25 _____   **32.** 14 ÷ 0.002 _____

33. 2,108.2 ÷ 83 _____   **34.** 38.424 ÷ 1.2 _____

35. 241.93 ÷ 13 _____   **36.** 8.888 ÷ 4.04 _____

37. 1.12 ÷ 0.08 _____   **38.** 246.75 ÷ 0.987 _____

39. 6.644 ÷ 3.02 _____   **40.** 7,433.89 ÷ 373 _____

Comparing Fractions and Rounding Mixed Numbers

Finding a Common Denominator

Which is greater, $\frac{2}{3}$ or $\frac{3}{5}$?

First, find a common denominator.

Write some multiples of 3: 3, 6, 9, 12, 15, 18
Write some multiples of 5: 5, 10, 15, 20, 25, 30
A common multiple is 15.

Use 15 as a common denominator to express equivalent fractions.

$$15 \div 3 = 5 \qquad\qquad 15 \div 5 = 3$$

$$\frac{2}{3} = \frac{2 \times 5}{3 \times 5} = \frac{10}{15} \qquad \frac{3}{5} = \frac{3 \times 3}{5 \times 3} = \frac{9}{15}$$

$$\frac{10}{15} > \frac{9}{15}, \text{ so } \frac{2}{3} > \frac{3}{5}$$

An alternate method is to use cross products.

Multiply first numerator by second denominator.
Multiply first denominator by second numerator.

First product: $2 \times 5 = 10$
Second Product: $3 \times 3 = 9$

$$\begin{array}{cccccc} 10 & > & 9 & \text{so} & \frac{2}{3} & > & \frac{3}{5} \\ \text{first} & & \text{second} & & \text{first} & & \text{second} \\ \text{product} & & \text{product} & & \text{fraction} & & \text{fraction} \end{array}$$

Choose a common denominator for each pair of fractions.

1. $\frac{1}{2}$ and $\frac{4}{7}$ **a.** 22   **b.** 14   **c.** 34   _____

2. $\frac{8}{9}$ and $\frac{7}{8}$ **a.** 72   **b.** 36   **c.** 64   _____

3. $\frac{1}{6}$ and $\frac{1}{8}$ **a.** 32   **b.** 24   **c.** 16   _____

Which is greater?

4. $\frac{5}{9}$ and $\frac{6}{10}$ _____   5. $\frac{2}{3}$ or $\frac{21}{30}$ _____   6. $\frac{3}{8}$ or $\frac{5}{11}$ _____

Which is less?

7. $\frac{2}{3}$ or $\frac{5}{6}$ _____   8. $\frac{8}{9}$ or $\frac{23}{27}$ _____   9. $\frac{3}{7}$ or $\frac{3}{6}$ _____

Fractions

Comparing Fractions and Rounding Mixed Numbers

What were Sydney Carton's famous last words as he stepped to the guillotine in Charles Dickens's *Tale of Two Cities*?

To solve:

1. Work each exercise.
2. In the clue box find the word that matches each answer.
3. Write that word above the number of the exercise below.

Example: Which is greater?   **1.** $\frac{1}{7}$ or $\frac{1}{6}$

Solution: $\frac{1}{6}$ The word *that* matches $\frac{1}{6}$.
Write *that* above 1.

$\frac{2}{3}$—to	$\frac{1}{6}$—that
$\frac{5}{16}$—ever	$\frac{5}{8}$—is
$\frac{3}{5}$—have	$\frac{3}{4}$—than
$\frac{9}{16}$—a	$\frac{4}{5}$—go
$\frac{1}{4}$—known	$\frac{11}{15}$—rest
$\frac{9}{10}$—far	$\frac{13}{15}$—it
13—is	14—I
15—better	16—try

Which is greater?

2. $\frac{3}{4}$ or $\frac{2}{3}$ _____

3. $\frac{5}{16}$ or $\frac{1}{4}$ _____

4. $\frac{7}{10}$ or $\frac{4}{5}$ _____

Which is less?

5. $\frac{5}{8}$ or $\frac{11}{16}$ _____

6. $\frac{3}{4}$ or $\frac{3}{5}$ _____

7. $\frac{4}{5}$ or $\frac{11}{15}$ _____

Which is greatest?

8. $\frac{2}{3}$, $\frac{1}{2}$, or $\frac{2}{5}$ _____

9. $\frac{3}{4}$, $\frac{4}{5}$, or $\frac{9}{10}$ _____

10. $\frac{13}{15}$, $\frac{7}{10}$, or $\frac{2}{3}$ _____

Which is least?

11. $\frac{9}{16}$, $\frac{5}{8}$, or $\frac{3}{4}$ _____

12. $\frac{1}{2}$, $\frac{1}{3}$, or $\frac{1}{4}$ _____

13. $\frac{19}{20}$, $\frac{9}{10}$, or $\frac{23}{25}$ _____

Round to the nearest whole number.

14. $14\frac{17}{32}$ _____

15. $14\frac{12}{25}$ _____

16. $13\frac{9}{17}$ _____

"IT IS A FAR, FAR BETTER THING THAT I DO THAN I HAVE EVER DONE;

_____ _____ _____ _____ , _____ _____ _____ THAT
   10   5   11   13   9   14   7   1

_____ _____ _____ _____ , _____ _____ _____ ."
   15   4   8   2   16   6   3   12

Fractions

Expressing Fractions in Lowest Terms

Determining the Greatest Common Factor

Express $\frac{18}{24}$ in lowest terms.

First, find the greatest common factor (GCF).

Write the factors of 18: 1 2 3 6 9 18
Write the factors of 24: 1 2 3 4 6 8 12 24
The common factors are 1, 2, 3, 6.
The GCF is 6.

$\frac{18}{24} = \frac{18 \div 6}{24 \div 6} = \frac{3}{4}$ Divide both numerator and denominator by 6.

Check: $\frac{3}{4} = \frac{3 \times 6}{4 \times 6} = \frac{18}{24}$

Find all the factors of each number, then name the GCF of each pair of numbers.

1. 36: _____

   48: _____   GCF = _____

2. 42: _____

   77: _____   GCF = _____

3. 34: _____

   85: _____   GCF = _____

4. 45: _____

   120: _____   GCF = _____

Find the GCF of each pair of numbers.

5. 39 and 104 _____   6. 48 and 112 _____

7. 45 and 54 _____   8. 54 and 72 _____

Express each fraction in lowest terms.

9. $\frac{63}{72}$ _____   10. $\frac{24}{36}$ _____

11. $\frac{60}{135}$ _____   12. $\frac{25}{100}$ _____

13. $\frac{40}{240}$ _____   14. $\frac{25}{75}$ _____

Fractions

Expressing Fractions in Lowest Terms

Prime Factors

If the numbers in the numerator and denominator of a fraction are very large, it can be difficult to express the fraction in lowest terms. Often, it is easiest to start by finding the prime factors of the numbers in the numerator and denominator.

Example: Express $\frac{400}{1,850}$ in lowest terms.

Solution: First, use a factor tree to find the prime factors of both numbers.

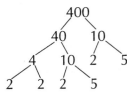

The prime factors
of 400 are
$2 \times 2 \times 2 \times 2 \times 5 \times 5$.

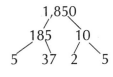

The prime factors
of 1,850 are
$2 \times 5 \times 5 \times 37$.

Find the common prime factors of both numbers.

$$400 = \boxed{2} \times 2 \times 2 \times 2 \times \boxed{5} \times \boxed{5}$$
$$1,850 = \boxed{2} \times \qquad \boxed{5} \times \boxed{5} \times 37$$

Multiply the common prime factors.
$2 \times 5 \times 5 = 50$
The GCF of 400 and 1,850 is 50.

Express $\frac{400}{1,850}$ in lowest terms using the GCF 50.

$$\frac{400}{1,850} = \frac{400 \div 50}{1,850 \div 50} = \frac{8}{37}$$

Use prime factorization to express each fraction in lowest terms.

1. $\frac{168}{420}$ ____

2. $\frac{315}{980}$ ____

3. $\frac{756}{954}$ ____

4. $\frac{765}{1,122}$ ____

5. $\frac{325}{1,175}$ ____

6. $\frac{672}{714}$ ____

7. $\frac{266}{1,444}$ ____

8. $\frac{945}{1,440}$ ____

9. $\frac{132}{209}$ ____

10. $\frac{296}{2,775}$ ____

11. $\frac{756}{1,113}$ ____

12. $\frac{1,344}{1,400}$ ____

Fractions

Improper Fractions and Mixed Numbers

Writing Mixed Numbers after Dividing Improper Fractions

Express $\frac{12}{8}$ as a mixed number.

First, divide the numerator (12)
by the denominator (8).

$$
\begin{array}{r}
1 \leftarrow \text{whole part} \\
8\overline{)12} \\
\underline{8} \\
4 \leftarrow \text{numerator of fraction}
\end{array}
$$

denominator of fraction

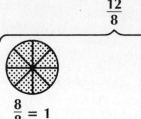

$\frac{8}{8} = 1$ $\frac{4}{8} = \frac{1}{2}$

The quotient 1 becomes the whole number part of the mixed number.
The remainder 4 becomes the numerator of the fractional part.
The divisor 8 becomes the denominator of the fractional part.

$\frac{12}{8} = 1\frac{4}{8} = 1\frac{1}{2}$ | Be sure to simplify. |

**Choose the correct division needed to express each improper
fraction as a mixed number.**

1. $\frac{13}{5}$ **a.** $5\overline{)13}$ **b.** $13\overline{)5}$ _____

2. $\frac{43}{6}$ **a.** $43\overline{)6}$ **b.** $6\overline{)43}$ _____

3. $\frac{30}{8}$ **a.** $8\overline{)30}$ **b.** $30\overline{)8}$ _____

**Express each improper fraction as a whole number or mixed
number.**

5. $\frac{16}{4}$ _____   6. $\frac{18}{11}$ _____   7. $\frac{16}{9}$ _____

8. $\frac{25}{4}$ _____   9. $\frac{26}{8}$ _____   10. $\frac{90}{27}$ _____

11. $\frac{15}{6}$ _____   12. $\frac{32}{5}$ _____   13. $\frac{52}{7}$ _____

Express each mixed number in simplest form.

14. $14\frac{12}{6}$ _____   15. $12\frac{15}{20}$ _____   16. $6\frac{8}{12}$ _____

17. $34\frac{5}{4}$ _____   18. $8\frac{17}{8}$ _____   19. $4\frac{21}{14}$ _____

Fractions

Improper Fractions and Mixed Numbers

Mixed Numbers

Solve each exercise. Then find each answer on the ruler below.
Write the letter that matches each answer above the number of
the exercise. The completed sentence is a difficult tongue twister.

1. $\frac{37}{8} = \underline{4\frac{5}{8}}$

2. $20 \div 10 = \underline{\hspace{1cm}}$

3. $\frac{11}{8} = \underline{\hspace{1cm}}$

4. $9 \div 2 = \underline{\hspace{1cm}}$

5. $27 \times \frac{1}{12} = \underline{\hspace{1cm}}$

6. $\frac{45}{8} = \underline{\hspace{1cm}}$

7. $\frac{53}{8} = \underline{\hspace{1cm}}$

8. $\frac{110}{16} = \underline{\hspace{1cm}}$

9. $36 \div 8 = \underline{\hspace{1cm}}$

10. $\frac{18}{8} = \underline{\hspace{1cm}}$

11. $9 \times \frac{1}{8} = \underline{\hspace{1cm}}$

12. $\frac{11}{4} = \underline{\hspace{1cm}}$

13. $51 \div 8 = \underline{\hspace{1cm}}$

14. $100 \div 50 = \underline{\hspace{1cm}}$

15. $\frac{22}{16} = \underline{\hspace{1cm}}$

16. $36 \div 16 = \underline{\hspace{1cm}}$

17. $\frac{44}{16} = \underline{\hspace{1cm}}$

18. $\frac{90}{20} = \underline{\hspace{1cm}}$

19. $\frac{102}{16} = \underline{\hspace{1cm}}$

20. $\frac{45}{20} = \underline{\hspace{1cm}}$

21. $\frac{90}{16} = \underline{\hspace{1cm}}$

22. $74 \div 16 = \underline{\hspace{1cm}}$

23. $\frac{98}{49} = \underline{\hspace{1cm}}$

24. $18 \times \frac{1}{4} = \underline{\hspace{1cm}}$

25. $\frac{55}{8} = \underline{\hspace{1cm}}$

26. $33 \div 24 = \underline{\hspace{1cm}}$

27. $44 \times \frac{1}{32} = \underline{\hspace{1cm}}$

28. $\frac{60}{16} \underline{\hspace{1cm}}$

29. $54 \times \frac{1}{12} = \underline{\hspace{1cm}} \cdot$

30. $204 \div 32 = \underline{\hspace{1cm}}$

31. $36 \times \frac{1}{16} = \underline{\hspace{1cm}}$

32. $18 \times \frac{1}{16} = \underline{\hspace{1cm}}$

33. $88 \div 32 = \underline{\hspace{1cm}}$

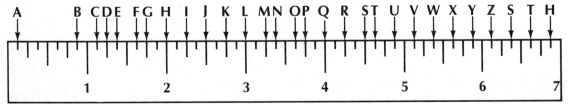

T _ _ _   _ _ _ _   _ _ _ _   _ _ _ _ _ _
1 2 3   4 5 6 7 8   9 10 11 12   13 14 15 16 17 18

_ _ _ _ _   _ _ _ _ _   _ _ _ _ .
19 20 21 22 23   24 25 26 27 28 29   30 31 32 33

Fractions

Fractional Parts of Numbers

Name three of the longest rivers in the world outside the United States.

To solve:

1. Work each exercise.
2. Look at the fractional part of each answer. Find the numerator to the left of the answer box. Find the denominator below the answer box.
3. Write the letter of the exercise in the box at the intersection of the row and column.

Example: Solve.   **L.**   What part of 5 is 1?

Solution: $\frac{1}{5}$ Write *L* in the box at the intersection of 1 and 5.

Solve.

A. What part of 8 is 7? _____

Z. What part of 16 is 7? _____

O. 7 is what part of 32? _____

A. 7 is what part of 13? _____

Y. What part of 64 is 5? _____

T. 5 is what part of 32? _____

B. What part of 32 is 20? _____

R. 15 is what part of 48? _____

Compare.

M. 7 with 11 _____

S. 10 with 144 _____

N. 45 with 10 _____

I. 14 with 56 _____

N. 135 with 64 _____

I. 18 with 13 _____

O. 25 with 30 _____

H. 86 with 81 _____

E. 14 with 12 _____

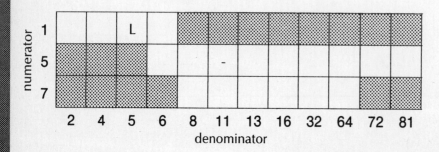

Least Common Denominator

Finding the Least Common Denominator

Find the least common denominator (LCD) of $\frac{3}{4}$ and $\frac{5}{6}$.
Then express $\frac{3}{4}$ and $\frac{5}{6}$ as equivalent fractions using the LCD.

To find the LCD, first find common multiples of the denominators.

4: 0, 4, 8, 12, 16, 20, 24, 28, 32, 36
6: 0, 6, 12, 18, 24, 30, 36

12, 24, and 36 are all common multiples of 4 and 6. But 12 is the least common multiple, so 12 is the least common denominator of $\frac{3}{4}$ and $\frac{5}{6}$.

Express $\frac{3}{4}$ and $\frac{5}{6}$ as equivalent fractions with the LCD (12).

$12 \div 4 = 3$ $12 \div 6 = 2$

$\frac{3}{4} = \frac{3 \times 3}{4 \times 3} = \frac{9}{12}$ $\frac{5}{6} = \frac{5 \times 2}{6 \times 2} = \frac{10}{12}$

Choose the LCD.

1. $\frac{1}{2}$ and $\frac{2}{3}$ **a.** 2   **b.** 3   **c.** 6   **d.** 12   _____

2. $\frac{3}{5}$ and $\frac{11}{15}$ **a.** 5   **b.** 15   **c.** 75   **d.** 60   _____

3. $\frac{7}{8}$ and $\frac{5}{6}$ **a.** 8   **b.** 48   **c.** 12   **d.** 24   _____

4. $\frac{3}{4}$ and $\frac{5}{14}$ **a.** 28   **b.** 14   **c.** 56   **d.** 112   _____

Find the LCD of the given fractions. Then express the given fractions as equivalent fractions using the LCD as their new denominator.

5. $\frac{1}{4}$ and $\frac{3}{8}$ _____

6. $\frac{1}{2}$ and $\frac{5}{6}$ _____

7. $\frac{11}{24}$ and $\frac{2}{3}$ _____

8. $\frac{7}{20}$ and $\frac{4}{5}$ _____

9. $\frac{2}{3}$ and $\frac{3}{4}$ _____

10. $\frac{4}{9}$ and $\frac{3}{8}$ _____

11. $\frac{7}{12}$ and $\frac{3}{8}$ _____

12. $\frac{1}{2}, \frac{2}{3}$, and $\frac{3}{5}$ _____

13. $\frac{1}{4}, \frac{3}{8}$, and $\frac{9}{16}$ _____

14. $\frac{2}{3}, \frac{1}{4}$, and $\frac{5}{8}$ _____

Fractions

Least Common Denominator

Equivalent Fractions Using LCD

To compare fractions with different denominators, rename each fraction using the least common denominator (LCD). Then compare their numerators.

Example: Choose the greatest fraction: $\frac{7}{9}$, $\frac{5}{6}$, or $\frac{2}{3}$.

Solution: Find the LCD.

9: 0, 9, ⑱ 27
6: 0, 6, 12, ⑱
3: 3, 6, 9, 12, 15, ⑱

The LCD is 18.

Write equivalent fractions using the LCD.

$\frac{7}{9} = \frac{14}{18}$ $\qquad$ $\frac{5}{6} = \frac{15}{18}$ $\qquad$ $\frac{2}{3} = \frac{12}{18}$

The greatest fraction is $\frac{5}{6}$.

Express the given fractions as equivalent fractions using the LCD. Then circle the greatest fraction.

1. $\frac{8}{9}$ $\frac{3}{4}$ $\frac{5}{6}$ $\frac{2}{3}$

Equivalent fractions: _____

2. $\frac{4}{5}$ $\frac{13}{16}$ $\frac{7}{8}$ $\frac{31}{40}$

Equivalent fractions: _____

3. $\frac{9}{14}$ $\frac{17}{35}$ $\frac{1}{2}$ $\frac{7}{10}$

Equivalent fractions: _____

4. $\frac{2}{3}$ $\frac{2}{7}$ $\frac{13}{14}$ $\frac{5}{6}$

Equivalent fractions: _____

5. $\frac{19}{21}$ $\frac{25}{28}$ $\frac{37}{42}$ $\frac{7}{12}$

Equivalent fractions: _____

6. $\frac{15}{48}$ $\frac{31}{32}$ $\frac{5}{12}$ $\frac{19}{24}$

Equivalent fractions: _____

7. $\frac{2}{3}$ $\frac{4}{5}$ $\frac{2}{10}$ $\frac{5}{6}$

Equivalent fractions: _____

8. $\frac{5}{8}$ $\frac{5}{6}$ $\frac{13}{18}$ $\frac{5}{9}$

Equivalent fractions: _____

9. $\frac{3}{25}$ $\frac{13}{75}$ $\frac{7}{50}$ $\frac{2}{15}$

Equivalent fractions: _____

10. $\frac{27}{33}$ $\frac{5}{6}$ $\frac{19}{22}$ $\frac{7}{11}$

Equivalent fractions: _____

11. $\frac{23}{52}$ $\frac{12}{13}$ $\frac{7}{26}$ $\frac{7}{8}$

Equivalent fractions: _____

12. $\frac{3}{4}$ $\frac{7}{12}$ $\frac{5}{6}$ $\frac{4}{9}$

Equivalent fractions: _____

Fractions

Expressing Fractions in Higher Terms

Finding Equivalent Fractions

Express $\frac{6}{8}$ as a fraction with a denominator of 24.

$$\frac{6}{8} = \frac{?}{24}$$

$$\frac{6 \times ?}{8 \times ?} = \frac{?}{24} \qquad \text{Think: What number times 8 equals 24? 3}$$

Multiply both numerator and denominator by 3 to find an equivalent fraction with a denominator of 24.

$$\frac{6 \times 3}{8 \times 3} = \frac{18}{24}$$

Choose the equivalent fraction with the specified denominator.

1. $\frac{2}{3}$ in 12ths   **a.** $\frac{2}{12}$ **b.** $\frac{4}{12}$ **c.** $\frac{8}{12}$ _____

2. $\frac{5}{8}$ in 16ths   **a.** $\frac{10}{16}$ **b.** $\frac{5}{16}$ **c.** $\frac{13}{16}$ _____

3. $\frac{1}{2}$ in 24ths   **a.** $\frac{1}{24}$ **b.** $\frac{12}{24}$ **c.** $\frac{3}{24}$ _____

4. $\frac{3}{5}$ in 20ths   **a.** $\frac{12}{20}$ **b.** $\frac{15}{20}$ **c.** $\frac{3}{20}$ _____

5. $\frac{7}{10}$ in 100ths   **a.** $\frac{700}{100}$ **b.** $\frac{70}{100}$ **c.** $\frac{7}{100}$ _____

6. $\frac{3}{4}$ in 200ths   **a.** $\frac{300}{200}$ **b.** $\frac{3}{200}$ **c.** $\frac{150}{200}$ _____

Complete.

7. $\frac{1}{6} = \frac{}{48}$ 8. $\frac{1}{11} = \frac{}{66}$ 9. $\frac{1}{5} = \frac{}{30}$

10. $\frac{5}{8} = \frac{}{32}$ 11. $\frac{3}{4} = \frac{}{16}$ 12. $\frac{5}{16} = \frac{}{96}$

13. $\frac{9}{20} = \frac{}{100}$ 14. $\frac{13}{25} = \frac{}{100}$ 15. $\frac{3}{10} = \frac{}{100}$

Express the following fractions as fractions having denominators as specified.

16. $\frac{5}{8}$ in 64ths _____   17. $\frac{1}{2}$ in 12ths _____   18. $\frac{3}{7}$ in 21sts _____

19. $\frac{4}{9}$ in 72nds _____   20. $\frac{7}{8}$ in 120ths _____   21. $\frac{19}{75}$ in 150ths _____

22. $\frac{7}{1}$ in 15ths _____   23. 15 in 30ths _____   24. 9 in 42nds _____

Fractions

Adding Fractions and Mixed Numbers

Addition of Fractions With Different Denominators

Add: $\frac{7}{8} + \frac{3}{5}$

To add fractions that do not have the same denominator, first express the fractions as equivalent fractions using the LCD. The LCD of $\frac{7}{8}$ and $\frac{3}{5}$ is 40.

$$\frac{7}{8} = \frac{7 \times 5}{8 \times 5} = \frac{35}{40}$$

$$\frac{3}{5} = \frac{3 \times 8}{5 \times 8} = \frac{24}{40}$$

Now add.

$$\begin{array}{r} \frac{35}{40} \\ + \frac{24}{40} \\ \hline \frac{59}{40} \end{array}$$

Add only the numerators. $35 + 24 = 59$
The denominator of the addends (the LCD) becomes the denominator of the sum.

Simplify. $\frac{59}{40} = 1\frac{19}{40}$

Choose the correct denominator to find the sum.

1. $\frac{3}{8} + \frac{5}{8}$ **a.** 16   **b.** 8   **c.** 5   _____

2. $\frac{1}{2} + \frac{1}{3}$ **a.** 2   **b.** 3   **c.** 6   _____

3. $\frac{5}{6} + \frac{7}{10}$ **a.** 30   **b.** 6   **c.** 10   _____

4. $5\frac{2}{3} + 6\frac{5}{6}$ **a.** 9   **b.** 6   **c.** 3   _____

Add.

5. $\begin{array}{r} \frac{3}{4} \\ + \frac{1}{2} \\ \hline \end{array}$

6. $\begin{array}{r} \frac{7}{18} \\ + \frac{1}{6} \\ \hline \end{array}$

7. $\begin{array}{r} \frac{3}{4} \\ + \frac{2}{5} \\ \hline \end{array}$

8. $\begin{array}{r} 7 \\ + \frac{6}{11} \\ \hline \end{array}$

9. $\begin{array}{r} 14 \\ + \frac{2}{3} \\ \hline \end{array}$

10. $\begin{array}{r} 3\frac{1}{2} \\ + 9\frac{2}{5} \\ \hline \end{array}$

11. $\begin{array}{r} 5\frac{2}{3} \\ + 7\frac{7}{8} \\ \hline \end{array}$

12. $\begin{array}{r} 11\frac{1}{10} \\ + 6\frac{7}{8} \\ \hline \end{array}$

13. $\begin{array}{r} 5\frac{7}{12} \\ + 7\frac{8}{15} \\ \hline \end{array}$

14. $\begin{array}{r} 6\frac{5}{6} \\ + 5\frac{7}{9} \\ \hline \end{array}$

15. $\begin{array}{r} 51\frac{7}{11} \\ + 48\frac{1}{3} \\ \hline \end{array}$

16. $\begin{array}{r} 16\frac{2}{3} \\ + 5\frac{1}{4} \\ \hline \end{array}$

17. $\begin{array}{r} 12\frac{7}{10} \\ + 18\frac{5}{12} \\ \hline \end{array}$

18. $\begin{array}{r} \frac{2}{3} \\ + \frac{11}{12} \\ \hline \end{array}$

19. $\begin{array}{r} \frac{3}{4} \\ + \frac{7}{16} \\ \hline \end{array}$

Fractions

Adding Fractions and Mixed Numbers

In 1783 two Frenchmen, Jacques and Joseph Montgolfier, built an aircraft. It was the first aircraft to lift human passengers into the air. What was it?

To solve:
1. Work each exercise.
2. Find each answer below.
3. Write the letter of the exercise above the answer.

Example: Add.   R. $\dfrac{1}{5}$

$+ \dfrac{1}{5}$

Solution: $\dfrac{2}{5}$ Write R above $\dfrac{2}{5}$.

Add.

N. $\dfrac{4}{5}$ L. $\dfrac{11}{16}$ A. $\dfrac{5}{12}$ T. $\dfrac{1}{4}$ O. $\dfrac{3}{8}$

$+\dfrac{3}{5}$ $+\dfrac{13}{16}$ $+\dfrac{3}{4}$ $+\dfrac{2}{5}$ $+\dfrac{5}{12}$

A. $2\dfrac{2}{5}$ B. $2\dfrac{2}{9}$ L. $4\dfrac{3}{8}$ I. $2\dfrac{5}{12}$ O. $3\dfrac{5}{7}$

$+\,5$ $+\,5\dfrac{5}{9}$ $+\,2\dfrac{1}{8}$ $+\,3\dfrac{7}{12}$ $+\,2\dfrac{6}{7}$

H. $\dfrac{5}{6} + \dfrac{1}{4}$ _____

O. $2\dfrac{5}{6} + \dfrac{2}{9} + 3\dfrac{1}{2}$ _____   A. $1\dfrac{1}{6} + 2\dfrac{2}{3} + 2\dfrac{5}{12}$ _____

___ ___ ___ ___   ___ ___ $\overset{R}{\underline{\quad}}$ ___ ___ ___ ___ ___ ___ ___

$7\dfrac{2}{5}$ $1\dfrac{1}{12}$ $6\dfrac{4}{7}$ $\dfrac{13}{20}$ $6\dfrac{1}{4}$ 6 $\dfrac{2}{5}$ $7\dfrac{7}{9}$ $1\dfrac{1}{6}$ $6\dfrac{1}{2}$ $1\dfrac{1}{2}$ $\dfrac{19}{24}$ $6\dfrac{5}{9}$ $1\dfrac{2}{5}$

Fractions

Subtracting Fractions and Mixed Numbers

Subtract: $5\frac{3}{8} - 2\frac{1}{2}$

To subtract fractions that do not have the same denominator,
first express the fractions as equivalent fractions using the LCD.
The LCD of $\frac{3}{8}$ and $\frac{1}{2}$ is 8.

$5\frac{3}{8} = 5\frac{3 \times 1}{8 \times 1} = 5\frac{3}{8}$

$2\frac{1}{2} = 2\frac{1 \times 4}{2 \times 4} = 2\frac{4}{8}$

Now subtract:

$5\frac{3}{8} = 4\frac{3}{8} + \frac{8}{8} = 4\frac{11}{8}$

$-2\frac{4}{8} \qquad = 2\frac{4}{8}$

$\qquad\qquad\qquad 2\frac{7}{8}$

Regroup 1 as $\frac{8}{8}$. $\frac{8}{8} + \frac{3}{8} = \frac{11}{8}$
Subtract the numerators. $11 - 4 = 7$
Subtract the whole numbers. $4 - 2 = 2$
The denominator remains the same.

Choose the correct denominator to find the difference.

1. $8\frac{3}{5} - 4\frac{1}{5}$ **a.** 10   **b.** 3   **c.** 5   _____

2. $\frac{11}{12} - \frac{7}{16}$ **a.** 48   **b.** 16   **c.** 12   _____

3. $6 - 4\frac{3}{4}$ **a.** 2   **b.** 4   **c.** 6   _____

4. $12\frac{1}{3} - 8\frac{5}{6}$ **a.** 6   **b.** 9   **c.** 3   _____

Subtract.

5. $\quad\frac{11}{12}$
$\quad -\frac{7}{9}$

6. $\quad\frac{15}{16}$
$\quad -\frac{5}{12}$

7. $\quad\frac{5}{6}$
$\quad -\frac{1}{3}$

8. $\quad\frac{3}{4}$
$\quad -\frac{1}{5}$

9. $\quad 12\frac{13}{15}$
$\quad -9\frac{3}{5}$

10. $\quad 36\frac{4}{5}$
$\quad -21\frac{1}{2}$

11. $\quad 27$
$\quad -18\frac{7}{11}$

12. $\quad 11\frac{1}{3}$
$\quad -\frac{7}{9}$

13. $\quad 21\frac{5}{16}$
$\quad -15\frac{11}{32}$

Fractions

Subtracting Fractions and Mixed Numbers

Name the Russian writer who won the Nobel Prize for Literature in 1970 and was deported from the Soviet Union in 1974.

To solve:

1. Work each exercise.
2. Look at the fractional part of each answer. Find the numerator to the left of the clue box. Find the denominator below the clue box. Find the letter at the intersection of the row and column.
3. Write that letter above the number of the exercise each time it appears below.

numerator							
1	E	F	O	R	O	Y	A	A
2	C	R	P	Z	E	S	S	J
3	V	R	N	I	T	L	H	W
4	B	D	E	K	C	S	T	Q
5	E	T	R	M	L	D	H	A

| 2 | 3 | 4 | 5 | 6 | 8 | 9 | 12 |

denominator

Example: Subtract.   **1.** $\dfrac{5}{9} - \dfrac{4}{9}$

Solution: $\dfrac{1}{9}$ The letter at the intersection of 1 and 9 is A. Write A above 1.

Subtract and simplify.

2. $\dfrac{5}{8}$
$-\dfrac{1}{8}$

3. $\dfrac{5}{8}$
$-\dfrac{1}{4}$

4. $\dfrac{5}{6}$
$-\dfrac{3}{4}$

5. $8\dfrac{7}{9}$
$-\dfrac{1}{3}$

6. $4\dfrac{7}{12}$
$-1\dfrac{5}{12}$

7. $3\dfrac{2}{5}$
$-1\dfrac{3}{5}$

8. $6\dfrac{5}{8}$
$-1\dfrac{7}{8}$

9. $7\dfrac{5}{9}$
-3

10. 7
$-3\dfrac{7}{8}$

11. $6\dfrac{11}{12}$
$-2\dfrac{1}{4}$

12. $4\dfrac{5}{6}$
$-1\dfrac{1}{12}$

13. $6\dfrac{5}{9}$
$-\dfrac{1}{18}$

14. $3\dfrac{1}{2}$
$-1\dfrac{2}{3}$

15. $6\dfrac{1}{2}$
$-2\dfrac{9}{10}$

16. $8\dfrac{1}{4}$
$-2\dfrac{17}{20}$

17. $5\dfrac{15}{16}$
$-5\dfrac{3}{16}$

18. 7
$-\dfrac{3}{8}$

19. $\dfrac{35}{36}$
$-\dfrac{3}{4}$

___ ___ ___ ___ ___ $\overset{A}{\_\_\_}$ ___ ___ ___
  4   3   2   7   19   1   12   18   11

___ ___ ___ ___ ___ ___ ___ ___ ___ ___ ___
 19   6   14   16   9   13   17   15   5   19   10   8

51

Fractions

Writing Mixed Numbers as Improper Fractions

Understanding Improper Fractions

Write $2\frac{1}{3}$ as an improper fraction.

Use a picture to help.

$2\frac{1}{3} = \frac{?}{3}$

Think: How many thirds
are equal to $2\frac{1}{3}$?

Rewrite $2\frac{1}{3}$ as $1 + 1 + \frac{1}{3}$.

Rewrite 1 as $\frac{3}{3}$.

$2\frac{1}{3} = 1 + 1 + \frac{1}{3} = \frac{3}{3} + \frac{3}{3} + \frac{1}{3} = \frac{7}{3}$

$$\frac{3}{3} + \frac{3}{3} + \frac{1}{3} = \frac{7}{3}$$

You can also use a shortcut.

To write a mixed number, as an improper fraction, multiply the denominator (3) by the whole number part (2) and add the numerator of the fraction (1). This result $(2 \times 3 + 1 = 7)$ becomes the numerator of the improper fraction. Keep the same denominator as in the mixed number (3).

number of thirds in 2

$2\frac{1}{3} = \frac{(2 \times 3) + 1}{3} = \frac{7}{3}$

Shade the picture to represent each mixed number. Then write the mixed number as an improper fraction.

1. $2\frac{1}{2}$

 $2\frac{1}{2} =$ _____

2. $3\frac{5}{8}$

 $3\frac{5}{8} =$ _____

3. $1\frac{4}{5}$

 $1\frac{4}{5} =$ _____

4. $2\frac{3}{4}$

 $2\frac{3}{4} =$ _____

Write each mixed number as an improper fraction.

5. $1\frac{1}{2}$ ——

6. $1\frac{5}{6}$ ——

7. $1\frac{7}{15}$ ——

8. $1\frac{12}{19}$ ——

9. $7\frac{1}{3}$ ——

10. $9\frac{7}{8}$ ——

Fractions

Multiplying Fractions and Mixed Numbers

Dividing by the GCF

Multiply: $6\frac{2}{3} \times 1\frac{1}{5}$

First, express any mixed numbers as improper fractions.

$6\frac{2}{3} \times 1\frac{1}{5} = \frac{20}{3} \times \frac{6}{5}$

Divide the numerators and denominators by their greatest common factor.
Every time you divide a numerator, you must divide a denominator by the same number.
Circle the factors that are left.

$\frac{20}{\cancel{3}} \times \frac{\cancel{6}}{5}$ Divide 3 and 6 by 3.

$\frac{\cancel{20}}{\cancel{3}} \times \frac{\cancel{6}}{\cancel{5}}$ Divide 20 and 5 by 5.

$\frac{\cancel{20}}{\cancel{3}} = \frac{\cancel{6}}{\cancel{5}} = \frac{4 \times 2}{1 \times 1} = \frac{8}{1} = 8$ Multiply the remaining factors in the numerator and the denominator.
Don't forget factors of 1.

Choose an equivalent multiplication.

1. $\frac{2}{5} \times \frac{5}{14}$ a. $\frac{1 \times 1}{5 \times 7}$ b. $\frac{1 \times 1}{1 \times 7}$ c. $\frac{2 \times 5}{1 \times 7}$ _____

2. $\frac{4}{9} \times 18$ a. $\frac{4 \times 2}{1 \times 1}$ b. $\frac{1 \times 2}{3 \times 1}$ c. $\frac{4 \times 1}{1 \times 1}$ _____

3. $6 \times \frac{2}{3}$ a. $\frac{2 \times 2}{1 \times 3}$ b. $\frac{2 \times 1}{1 \times 1}$ c. $\frac{2 \times 2}{1 \times 1}$ _____

4. $1\frac{1}{2} \times 1\frac{5}{9}$ a. $\frac{3 \times 7}{1 \times 1}$ b. $\frac{1 \times 7}{1 \times 3}$ c. $\frac{1 \times 7}{2 \times 3}$ _____

5. $4\frac{1}{5} \times \frac{2}{3}$ a. $\frac{7 \times 2}{5 \times 1}$ b. $\frac{7 \times 1}{5 \times 3}$ c. $\frac{4 \times 2}{1 \times 3}$ _____

6. $\frac{6}{25} \times \frac{5}{12}$ a. $\frac{1 \times 1}{5 \times 3}$ b. $\frac{1 \times 5}{5 \times 2}$ c. $\frac{1 \times 1}{5 \times 2}$ _____

Multiply.

7. $\frac{1}{7} \times \frac{1}{3}$ _____

8. $\frac{7}{8} \times \frac{5}{6}$ _____

9. $\frac{9}{14} \times 7$ _____

10. $8 \times \frac{4}{5}$ _____

11. $\frac{4}{9} \times 6\frac{3}{4}$ _____

12. $1\frac{1}{7} \times 4\frac{2}{3}$ _____

Fractions

Multiplying Fractions and Mixed Numbers

One type of bird builds a nest shaped like a teepee and taller than a human. Inside, the bird constructs several rooms and decorates them with shells, berries, and flowers. What bird is it?

To solve:
1. Work each exercise.
2. In the clue box find the letter that matches each answer.
3. Write that letter above the number of the exercise each time it appears below.

$\frac{1}{12}$—S	$\frac{1}{8}$—R
$\frac{6}{35}$—E	$\frac{1}{4}$—R
$\frac{5}{14}$—T	$\frac{2}{3}$—B
$1\frac{3}{4}$—L	$2\frac{1}{10}$—E
$3\frac{1}{3}$—B	$3\frac{3}{4}$—I
$4\frac{1}{5}$—E	6—C
$6\frac{2}{3}$—D	$11\frac{2}{3}$—D
$17\frac{1}{3}$—W	18—A
20—O	21—G
$28\frac{1}{2}$—S	$7\frac{1}{5}$—N

Example: Multiply. **1.** $\frac{1}{3} \times \frac{1}{4}$

Solution: $\frac{1}{12}$ S matches $\frac{1}{12}$. Write S above 1.

Multiply.

2. $\frac{2}{5} \times \frac{3}{7}$ _____

3. $\frac{3}{4} \times \frac{1}{3}$ _____

4. $\frac{5}{12} \times \frac{6}{7}$ _____

5. $\frac{11}{12} \times \frac{8}{11}$ _____

6. $\frac{5}{2} \times \frac{8}{3}$ _____

7. $\frac{3}{8} \times 4\frac{2}{3}$ _____

8. $2\frac{5}{8} \times 2\frac{2}{7}$ _____

9. $\frac{5}{16} \times 12$ _____

10. $\frac{7}{10} \times 3$ _____

11. $16 \times \frac{5}{4}$ _____

12. $12 \times 2\frac{3}{8}$ _____

13. $5 \times 2\frac{1}{3}$ _____

14. $2\frac{1}{4} \times 8$ _____

15. $2\frac{1}{6} \times 8$ _____

16. $2\frac{2}{5} \times 3$ _____

17. $\frac{3}{4} \times \frac{2}{7} \times \frac{7}{12}$ _____

18. $\frac{7}{100} \times 300$ _____

19. Simplify: $\frac{20 \times 50}{25 \times 12}$ _____

20. Solve: $\frac{6}{5} \times \frac{7}{2} = n$ _____

__ __ __ __ __ __ __ __ S
8 17 10 12 4 7 20 12 1

__ __ __ __ __ __ __ __
18 14 17 13 2 16 20 3

__ __ __ __ __ __ __ __ __
19 11 15 2 3 5 9 17 6

Dividing Fractions and Mixed Numbers

Inverting the Divisor

Divide: $3\frac{2}{3} \div \frac{5}{6}$

First, express any mixed numbers as improper fractions.

$3\frac{2}{3} \div \frac{5}{6} = \frac{11}{3} \div \frac{5}{6}$

$\frac{11}{3} \times \frac{6}{5}$ Invert the divisor and change ÷ to ×.
Remember, the divisor is always the second number.

$\frac{11}{3} \times \frac{6}{5}$ Divide the numerators and denominators by their
greatest common factor.
Divide 3 and 6 by 3.

Now multiply.

$\frac{11}{3} \times \frac{6}{5} = \frac{11 \times 2}{1 \times 5} = \frac{22}{5} = 4\frac{2}{5}$

> Don't forget to change improper fractions to mixed numbers.

Choose the multiplication problem which is equivalent to the given division problem.

1. $\frac{7}{8} \div \frac{5}{6}$ a. $\frac{7}{8} \times \frac{6}{5}$ b. $\frac{8}{7} \times \frac{6}{5}$ c. $\frac{8}{7} \times \frac{5}{6}$ _____

2. $7\frac{3}{4} \div 5$ a. $\frac{4}{31} \times 5$ b. $\frac{31}{4} \times \frac{1}{5}$ c. $\frac{31}{4} \times 5$ _____

3. $\frac{3}{5} \div 1\frac{1}{2}$ a. $\frac{3}{5} \times \frac{3}{2}$ b. $\frac{5}{3} \times \frac{3}{2}$ c. $\frac{3}{5} \times \frac{2}{3}$ _____

4. $5\frac{1}{3} \div 4\frac{1}{5}$ a. $\frac{16}{3} \times \frac{5}{21}$ b. $\frac{3}{16} \times \frac{21}{5}$ c. $\frac{16}{3} \times \frac{21}{5}$ _____

Divide.

5. $\frac{3}{4} \div \frac{6}{7}$ _____

6. $\frac{5}{11} \div \frac{13}{22}$ _____

7. $\frac{1}{2} \div \frac{3}{4}$ _____

8. $\frac{3}{4} \div \frac{5}{8}$ _____

9. $\frac{5}{6} \div 2$ _____

10. $\frac{10}{18} \div 5$ _____

11. $6 \div \frac{3}{5}$ _____

12. $6 \div \frac{3}{17}$ _____

13. $2\frac{1}{2} \div \frac{5}{8}$ _____

14. $\frac{7}{11} \div 4\frac{1}{5}$ _____

15. $6\frac{1}{3} \div 3\frac{2}{3}$ _____

16. $4\frac{1}{5} \div 3\frac{5}{10}$ _____

17. $4\frac{1}{8} \div 4\frac{2}{5}$ _____

18. $3\frac{3}{16} \div 2\frac{1}{8}$ _____

Fractions

Dividing Fractions and Mixed Numbers

**The man who led the 1810 revolt to free
Mexico from Spain was a priest. Name him.**

To solve:

1. Work each exercise.
2. Find each answer below. Write the letter of the exercise above
   the answer.

Example: Divide. **L.** $\frac{1}{2} \div \frac{2}{3}$

Solution: $\frac{3}{4}$ Write L above $\frac{3}{4}$.

Divide.

I. $\frac{4}{5} \div \frac{3}{8}$ _____

S. $\frac{7}{8} \div \frac{5}{12}$ _____

L. $10 \div \frac{3}{4}$ _____

A. $60 \div 4\frac{2}{7}$ _____

D. $8\frac{1}{4} \div 1\frac{3}{8}$ _____

G. $\frac{4}{7} \div 1\frac{1}{7}$ _____

H. $8\frac{1}{6} \div \frac{7}{15}$ _____

C. Simplify: $\dfrac{\frac{3}{4}}{\frac{2}{3}}$ _____

E. $\frac{5}{8} \div \frac{15}{16}$ _____

Y. $\frac{4}{5} \div 12$ _____

U. $2\frac{3}{4} \div 11$ _____

T. $5 \div 9\frac{1}{6}$ _____

A. $5\frac{1}{7} \div 1\frac{6}{21}$ _____

L. $\frac{7}{10} \div 2\frac{3}{4}$ _____

O. Solve: $n = 14 \div 5\frac{1}{4}$ _____

I. $\frac{5}{7} \div \frac{5}{21}$ _____

I. $9 \div \frac{1}{3}$ _____

M. $6\frac{3}{4} \div 3$ _____

O. $1 \div 4\frac{1}{4}$ _____

L. $2\frac{3}{5} \div 26$ _____

G. $3\frac{2}{3} \div 4\frac{7}{12}$ _____

$\overline{}\ \overline{}\ \overline{}\ \overline{}\ \overline{}\ \overline{}\quad \overline{}\ \overline{}\ \overline{}\ \overline{}\ \overset{L}{\overline{}}\ \overline{}\ \overline{}$

$2\frac{1}{4}\quad 27\quad \frac{1}{2}\quad \frac{1}{4}\quad \frac{2}{3}\quad \frac{14}{55}\qquad 17\frac{1}{2}\quad 3\quad 6\quad 14\quad \frac{3}{4}\quad \frac{4}{5}\quad 2\frac{2}{3}$

$\overline{}\quad \overline{}\ \overline{}\ \overline{}\ \overline{}\ \overline{}\ \overline{}\ \overline{}$

$\frac{1}{15}\qquad 1\frac{1}{8}\quad \frac{4}{17}\quad 2\frac{1}{10}\quad \frac{6}{11}\quad 2\frac{2}{15}\quad \frac{1}{10}\quad 13\frac{1}{3}\quad 4$

Fractions

Writing Decimals as Fractions

Fujiyama is the highest mountain in Japan. What does its name mean?

To solve:
1. Work each exercise.
2. Look at the fractional part of each answer. Find the numerator to the left of the clue box. Find the denominator below the clue box. Find the letter at the intersection of the row and column.
3. Write that letter above the number of the exercise.

numerator	4	5	8	10	16	20
1	T	U	C	S	N	I
3	M	E	R	O	S	D
5	P	V	L	Z	T	M
7	O	C	A	N	E	K
9	N	H	Q	A	H	S

denominator

Example: Write the decimal as a fraction. **1.** 0.9

Solution: $\frac{9}{10}$ The letter at the intersection of 9 and 10 is *A*. Write *A* above 1.

Write each decimal as a fraction or mixed number.

2. 0.2 _____   **3.** 0.75 _____

4. 0.05 _____   **5.** 2.625 _____

6. 0.25 _____   **7.** 0.875 _____

8. 1.125 _____   **9.** 4.1 _____

10. 1.3125 _____   **11.** 0.7 _____

12. 0.5625 _____   **13.** 1.0625 _____

14. 2.3 _____   **15.** 8.4375 _____

16. 2.75 _____   **17.** 0.1875 _____

___ ___ ___ ___ ___ ___ ___ ___ ___   ___ ___ ___ ___ ___ A ___ ___
 3   7   6   8 12   5 15   9 17   16 14   2 11 10   1   4 13

57

Fractions

Writing Decimals as Fractions

Repeating Decimals

A decimal in which a digit or group of digits is repreated endlessly
is called a *repeating decimal*. The digit, or set of digits, with a bar
over it is repeated.

$\frac{1}{9} = 0.1111 \ldots = 0.\overline{1}$

Example: Write the repeating decimal 0.2949494949 . . . using a bar.

Solution: $0.2949494949494 \ldots = 0.2\overline{94}$

Repeating decimals can be written as fractions. Look at this
pattern.

$$0.\overline{1} = \frac{1}{9} \qquad 0.\overline{01} = \frac{1}{99} \qquad 0.\overline{001} = \frac{1}{999}$$

You can use multiples to write some repeating decimals as
fractions.

Example: Write each repeating decimal as a fraction.
   a. $0.\overline{8}$ **b.** $0.\overline{82}$ **c.** $0.\overline{824}$

Solution:
   a. $0.\overline{8} = 8 \times 0.\overline{1}$
      $= 8 \times \frac{1}{9}$
      $= \frac{8}{9}$

   b. $0.\overline{82} = 82 \times 0.\overline{01}$
      $= 82 \times \frac{1}{99}$
      $= \frac{82}{99}$

   c. $0.\overline{824} = 824 \times 0.\overline{001}$
      $= 824 \times \frac{1}{999}$
      $= \frac{824}{999}$

Write each repeating decimal using a bar.

1. 0.444 . . . _____   2. 5.8666 . . . _____   3. 12.8252525 . . . _____

Write each repeating decimal as a multiple of $0.\overline{1}$, $0.\overline{01}$, or $0.\overline{001}$.

4. 0.888 . . . _____   5. 0.585858 . . . _____   6. 0.171717 . . . _____

7. $0.\overline{651}$ _____   8. $0.\overline{7}$ _____   9. $0.\overline{25}$ _____

Write each repeating decimal as a fraction.

10. 0.222 . . . _____   11. $0.\overline{6}$ _____   12. 0.858585 . . . _____

13. $0.\overline{04}$ _____   14. $19.\overline{5}$ _____   15. 0.123123123 . . . _____

16. $2.\overline{8}$ _____   17. $0.\overline{13}$ _____   18. $8.\overline{06}$ _____

Fractions

Writing Fractions as Decimals

Writing Mixed Numbers as Decimals

Write $2\frac{3}{4}$ as a decimal.

First, write the mixed number as the sum of a whole number and a fraction.

$$2\frac{3}{4} = 2 + \frac{3}{4}$$

Then express the fraction as a decimal.
To express $\frac{3}{4}$ as a decimal, divide 3 by 4.

```
    0.75
4)3.00
   2 8
     20
     20
      0
```

$\frac{3}{4} = 0.75$, so $2 + \frac{3}{4} = 2 + 0.75 = 2.75$

$2\frac{3}{4} = 2.75$

Divide. Then write the decimal that is equal to the given fraction.

1. 5)3.0 $\frac{3}{5}$ = _____   2. 8)7.00 $\frac{7}{8}$ = _____

3. 10)7.00 $\frac{7}{10}$ = _____   4. 4)1.00 $\frac{1}{4}$ = _____

Write each fraction or mixed number as a decimal.

5. $8\frac{3}{10}$ _____   6. $3\frac{9}{10}$ _____   7. $\frac{82}{100}$ _____

8. $1\frac{4}{100}$ _____   9. $6\frac{2}{5}$ _____   10. $18\frac{16}{25}$ _____

11. $5\frac{7}{20}$ _____   12. $\frac{11}{50}$ _____   13. $\frac{11}{16}$ _____

14. $\frac{15}{60}$ _____   15. $\frac{165}{100}$ _____   16. $\frac{5\frac{1}{2}}{100}$ _____

17. $\frac{17}{8}$ _____   18. $\frac{21}{5}$ _____   19. $1\frac{3}{16}$ _____

20. $6\frac{2}{5}$ _____   21. $\frac{21}{16}$ _____   22. $\frac{21}{50}$ _____

23. $\frac{625}{1,000}$ _____   24. $\frac{127}{10,000}$ _____   25. $\frac{23}{8}$ _____

Fractions

Estimation/Mental Math

Carpenters, bakers, and decorators use fractions in their measurements. When they buy materials, however, they may need to use whole-number estimates.
The symbol "$\approx$" means "is about equal to." For example, $\frac{7}{8}$ "≈ 1" means $\frac{7}{8}$ "is about equal to 1."

Example: Estimate the difference. $10\frac{7}{8} - 3\frac{1}{50}$

Solution: $10\frac{7}{8} \approx 11 \qquad 3\frac{1}{50} \approx 3$

$11 - 3 = 8$
The difference is about 8.

Example: Estimate the sum. $6\frac{5}{16} + 2\frac{13}{16} + 7\frac{9}{10}$

Solution: $\frac{5}{16} + \frac{13}{16} \approx 1 \qquad \frac{9}{10} \approx 1$

$6 + 2 + 7 + 1 + 1 = 17$
The sum is about 17.

Estimate.

1. $25\frac{2}{5}$
$+ \ 3\frac{3}{10}$
_____

2. $11\frac{1}{16}$
$+ 20\frac{1}{100}$
_____

3. $8\frac{5}{9}$
$- 2\frac{1}{3}$
_____

4. $13\frac{1}{2}$
$- \ 9\frac{7}{40}$
_____

5. $2\frac{1}{4}$
$7\frac{11}{12}$
$+ 1\frac{3}{4}$
_____

6. $10\frac{1}{2}$
$9\frac{1}{20}$
$+ \ 5\frac{1}{2}$
_____

7. $3\frac{1}{5} \div \frac{4}{5}$ _____

8. $5\frac{5}{7} \div \frac{10}{21}$ _____

9. $5\frac{2}{3} \times 2\frac{1}{3}$ _____

10. $1\frac{1}{4} \times 12$ _____

11. $14\frac{5}{8} - 5\frac{1}{6}$ _____

12. $3\frac{1}{7} \div \frac{11}{14}$ _____

13. $50\frac{1}{3} - 13\frac{1}{2}$ _____

14. $1\frac{13}{15} \times \frac{9}{10}$ _____

15. $1\frac{2}{5} \times 5\frac{1}{2}$ _____

16. $9\frac{3}{8} + 14\frac{1}{4}$ _____

17. $3\frac{7}{8} \times 15$ _____

18. $8\frac{1}{4} - 5\frac{7}{8}$ _____

19. $13\frac{2}{3} - 1\frac{1}{2}$ _____

20. $4\frac{1}{5} \div \frac{7}{12}$ _____

21. The Space Age Dance Troupe has 12 members. Costumes for the two lead dancers require $1\frac{7}{8}$ yards of fabric each. Costumes for the other dancers require $1\frac{1}{2}$ yards each. Estimate to determine if 30 yards of fabric will be enough for a new set of costumes. _____

Fractions

NAME _____ CLASS _____ DATE _____

Meaning of Percent

In 1783, Benjamin Franklin wrote about war and peace. What did he say?

To solve:
1. Work each exercise.
2. Find each answer below.
3. Write the letter of the exercise above the answer each time it appears.

Example: Express the following as a percent.   **D.** 6 hundredths

Solution: 6%   Write *D* above 6%.

Express each of the following as a percent.

O. 45 hundredths _____   **A.** 125 hundredths _____   **A.** 1.4 out of 100 _____

Write the number of hundredths.

A. $12\frac{1}{2}\%$ _____   **R.** 60% _____   **R.** 4.5% _____

Write each of the following as a decimal.

W. forty-five hundredths _____   **A.** six hundredths _____

E. twelve hundredths _____   **C.** sixty hundredths _____

Write each of the following as a fraction.

P. forty-five hundredths _____   **O.** seventy-two hundredths _____

Write each percent as a ratio.

D. 91% _____   **G.** 9% _____   **B.** 400% _____

"THERE NEVER WAS A

_____ _____ _____ _____D_____   _____ _____ _____   _____ _____
9:100 $\frac{72}{100}$ 45% 6%   0.45 125% 60   45% 4.5

_____ _____ _____ _____   _____ _____ _____ _____ _____."
$12\frac{1}{2}$ 400:100 1.4% 91:100 $\frac{45}{100}$ 0.12 0.06 0.60 0.12

Meaning of Percent

Fractional Percent

Write $7\frac{2}{3}$ hundredths as a percent.

$7\frac{2}{3}$ hundredths

$7\frac{2}{3}\%$ Replace hundredths with %.

$7\frac{2}{3}$ hundredths $= 7\frac{2}{3}\%$

Remember, % means hundredths.

How many hundredths are in 19.5%?

19.5%
19.5 hundredths Replace % with hundredths.
19.5% = 19.5 hundredths

Choose the correct answer.

1. Write 21 hundredths as a percent.
   a. 0.2%   **b.** 21   **c.** 21% _____

2. Write $6\frac{1}{2}$ hundredths as a percent.
   a. $6\frac{1}{2}$ **b.** $6\frac{1}{2}\%$ **c.** $0.06\frac{1}{2}\%$ _____

3. How many hundredths are in 14.8%?
   a. 148   **b.** 14.8   **c.** 1.48 _____

Write each of the following as a percent.

4. 3 hundredths _____   5. $14\frac{1}{2}$ hundredths _____

6. $25\frac{3}{4}$ hundredths _____   7. $18\frac{1}{3}$ hundredths _____

Give the number of hundredths in each percent.

8. 5% _____   9. $56\frac{1}{2}\%$ _____   10. 100% _____   11. $\frac{1}{4}\%$ _____

Write each of the following as a percent, a decimal, and a fraction.

12. Twenty-three hundredths _____

13. 89 hundredths _____

NAME _____ CLASS _____ DATE _____

Writing Percents as Decimals

The largest known butterfly is found in Papua, New Guinea. Name it.

To solve:
1. Work each exercise.
2. In the clue box, find the letter that matches each answer.
3. Write that letter above the number of the exercise below.

0.625—E	0.8075—N
0.024—N	0.0625—L
1.005—U	1.49—I
0.08—E	0.24—A
1.80—R	0.50—X
0.725—B	0.018—E
0.0475—R	0.92—I
0.0875—G	1.50—D
2.40—A	0.80—Q
0.005—N	1.08—D
0.05—A	8.00—W

Example: Write the percent as a decimal. **1.** 5%

Solution: 0.05   The letter A matches 0.05. Write A above 1.

Write each percent as a decimal.

2. 8% _____

3. 24% _____

4. 92% _____

5. 50% _____

6. 80% _____

7. 149% _____

8. 108% _____

9. 150% _____

10. 180% _____

11. 800% _____

12. $62\frac{1}{2}$% _____

13. $6\frac{1}{4}$% _____

14. $1\frac{4}{5}$% _____

15. $80\frac{3}{4}$% _____

16. $100\frac{1}{2}$% _____

17. 2.4% _____

18. 8.75% _____

19. 240% _____

20. 72.5% _____

21. $4\frac{3}{4}$% _____

22. 0.5% _____

___ ___ ___ ___ ___   A ___ ___ ___ ___ ___ ___ ___ ___ ___
 6   16   2   12   15   1   13   14   5   3   22   8   10   19

___ ___ ___ ___ ___ ___ ___ ___
20   7   21   9   11   4   17   18

Writing Percents as Decimals

Decimal Point Placement

Write 156% as a decimal.

Remember, % means hundredths.

156% = 156 hundredths
156 hundredths = 1.56
156% = 1.56

As a shortcut, move the decimal point 2 places to the left and drop the percent sign.

Write 0.71% as a decimal.

0.71% = 0.71 hundredths
0.71 hundredths = 0.0071
0.71% = 0.0071

Move the decimal point 2 places to the left and drop the percent sign.

Choose the correct decimal equivalent.

1. 29%   **a.** 0.29   **b.** 0.29%   **c.** 29   _____

2. 8%   **a.** 8%   **b.** 0.8   **c.** 0.08   _____

3. 192%   **a.** 19.2   **b.** 192   **c.** 1.92   _____

4. 100%   **a.** 0.1   **b.** 1   **c.** 100   _____

5. 0.4%   **a.** 0.004   **b.** 0.04   **c.** 0.4   _____

6. 21.3%   **a.** 2.13   **b.** 0.213   **c.** 213%   _____

Write each percent as a decimal.

7. 25% _____   **8.** 17% _____   **9.** 83% _____

10. 5% _____   **11.** 2% _____   **12.** $6\frac{1}{2}$% _____

13. $210\frac{1}{2}$% _____   **14.** 308% _____   **15.** 101% _____

16. 7.9% _____   **17.** 82.3% _____   **18.** $12\frac{1}{4}$% _____

19. $1\frac{1}{2}$% _____   **20.** 0.7% _____   **21.** $\frac{3}{4}$% _____

22. $0.3\frac{1}{2}$% _____   **23.** 0.02% _____   **24.** 0.85% _____

NAME _____ CLASS _____ DATE _____

Writing Decimals as Percents

Decimal Point Placement

Write 0.8 as a percent.

    0.8 = 0.80 = 80 hundredths
    80 hundredths = 80%
    0.8 = 80%   Move the decimal point 2 places to
                             the right and write a percent sign.

Write 2.67 as a percent.

    2.67 = 267 hundredths
    267 hundredths = 267%
    2.67 = 267%   Move the decimal point 2 places to
                             the right and write a percent sign.

Choose the correct percent equivalent.

1. 0.05	**a.** 5	**b.** 0.05%	**c.** 5%	_____
2. 0.3	**a.** 0.3%	**b.** 30%	**c.** 3%	_____
3. 2	**a.** 200%	**b.** 2%	**c.** 200	_____
4. 0.025	**a.** 0.25%	**b.** 2.5%	**c.** 25%	_____
5. 0.525	**a.** 5.25%	**b.** 52.5%	**c.** 52.5	_____
6. 0.005	**a.** 0.5%	**b.** 5%	**c.** 0.05%	_____

Write each decimal as a percent.

7. 0.09 _____   **8.** 0.56 _____   **9.** 0.3 _____

10. 0.6 _____   **11.** 1.12 _____   **12.** 2.4 _____

13. 3 _____   **14.** 0.21 _____   **15.** 0.8825 _____

16. 1.515 _____   **17.** 0.811 _____   **18.** 0.0251 _____

19. 0.25 _____   **20.** 0.725 _____   **21.** 0.0005 _____

22. 0.00625 _____   **23.** 2.1 _____   **24.** 4.5 _____

Writing Decimals as Percents

The oldest printed book in existence is a Buddhist manuscript printed in 868 A.D. What is it called and where was it found?

To solve:
1. Work each exercise.
2. Find each answer below.
3. Write the letter of the exercise above the answer.

Example: Write the decimal as a percent.   **A.** 0.07

Solution: 7%   Write *A* above 7%.

Write each decimal as a percent.

A. 0.04 _____   **U.** 0.43 _____   **E.** 0.79 _____

H. 0.4 _____   **O.** 1.66 _____   **N.** 1.4 _____

U. 1.8 _____   **T.** 0.66 _____   **H.** 0.87 _____

U. 0.06 _____   **H.** 0.10 _____   **D.** 0.60 _____

I. 1.87 _____   **G.** 2.03 _____   **A.** 0.108 _____

C. 0.079 _____   **N.** 0.014 _____   **T.** 0.68 _____

M. 0.45 _____   **R.** 1.79 _____   **I.** 4.25 _____

N. 4 _____   **D.** 7 _____   **S.** 0.31 _____

N. 0.09 _____   **T.** 0.004 _____   **A.** 0.0079 _____

____ ____ ____   ____ ____ _A_ ____ ____ ____ ____
66% 87% 79%   700% 425% 7% 45% 166% 9% 60%

____ ____ ____ ____ ____:
31% 43% 68% 179% 0.79%

____ ____ ____ - ____ ____ ____ ____ ____,   ____ ____ ____ ____ ____
0.4% 180% 1.4%   40% 6%   4% 400% 203%   7.9% 10% 187% 140% 10.8%

NAME _____ CLASS _____ DATE _____

Writing Decimals as Percents

Percents Greater Than 100%

The whole of a quantity is represented by 100%. Any increase results in a quantity that is greater than 100% of the original amount.

For example, many states and cities add a sales tax to the selling price of some items. The customer pays 100% of the selling price, plus a sales tax that is a percent of the selling price.

Example: In Topville, a sales tax of 5% is added to the selling price of a car. Express the total cost of the car as a percent of the selling price.

Solution: 100% of selling price
             +   5% of selling price
                  105% of selling price
The total cost of the car is 105% of the selling price.

Solve.

1. Different sales tax percents are listed below. The total cost of an item includes the sales tax. Express the total cost as a percent of the selling price.

   a. 2% _____   **b.** 4% _____   **c.** 5% _____   **d.** 7% _____

   e. 3% _____   **f.** 9% _____   **g.** 8% _____   **h.** 6% _____

2. The enrollment of each class at East Oshkosh High School increased over last year's enrollment by the percents stated below. State the present enrollment of each class as a percent of last year's enrollment.

   a. Freshmen: 9% _____   **b.** Sophomores: 11% _____

   c. Juniors: 8% _____   **d.** Seniors: 6% _____

*3. The population of Centerville increased by 21% from 1970 to 1980. From 1980 to 1990, the population is expected to increase by 17% of the 1970 figure.

   a. What will be the percent of increase over the 20-year period from 1970 to

   1990? _____

   b. What percent of the 1970 population will the 1990 population be? _____

Percents and Proportions

Writing Percents as Fractions

Expressing Mixed Numbers as Percents

Write $8\frac{1}{2}\%$ as a fraction.

$8\frac{1}{2} = \frac{17}{2}$ Write the mixed number as an improper fraction.

$\frac{17}{2} \div 100$ Divide by 100.

$\frac{17}{2} \times \frac{1}{100} = \frac{17}{200}$ | Remember, to divide, you invert the divisor and multiply.

$8\frac{1}{2}\% = \frac{17}{200}$

Choose the computation you would use to change each percent to a fraction.

1. $1\frac{1}{2}\%$ a. $\frac{3}{2} \times 100$ b. $\frac{3}{2} \div 100$ c. $\frac{1}{2} \div 100$ _____

2. $11\frac{2}{3}\%$ a. $\frac{22}{3} \div 100$ b. $\frac{35}{3} \times 100$ c. $\frac{35}{3} \div 100$ _____

3. $35\frac{1}{2}\%$ a. $\frac{71}{2} \div 100$ b. $\frac{35}{2} \div 100$ c. $\frac{71}{2} \times 100$ _____

4. $15\frac{3}{4}\%$ a. $\frac{15}{4} \div 100$ b. $\frac{45}{4} \div 100$ c. $\frac{63}{4} \div 100$ _____

5. $42\frac{1}{2}\%$ a. $\frac{85}{2} \div 100$ b. $\frac{42}{2} \div 100$ c. $\frac{85}{2} \div \frac{1}{100}$ _____

Write each percent as a fraction or mixed number.

6. 45% _____   7. 28% _____   8. 20% _____

9. $16\frac{2}{3}\%$ _____   10. $40\frac{1}{2}\%$ _____   11. $18\frac{3}{4}\%$ _____

12. $62\frac{1}{2}\%$ _____   13. $11\frac{1}{9}\%$ _____   14. $9\frac{1}{11}\%$ _____

15. 7% _____   16. 14% _____   17. $\frac{1}{2}\%$ _____

18. 165% _____   19. $212\frac{1}{2}\%$ _____   20. $333\frac{1}{3}\%$ _____

21. 18% _____   22. $87\frac{1}{2}\%$ _____   23. $91\frac{2}{3}\%$ _____

24. 480% _____   25. 209% _____   26. $93\frac{3}{4}\%$ _____

NAME _____ CLASS _____ DATE _____

Writing Percents as Fractions

The first women's rights convention was held in New York State in 1848. Who organized the convention and where was it held?

To solve:

1. Work each exercise.
2. Look at the fractional part of each answer. Find the numerator to the left of the clue box. Find the denominator below the clue box. Find the letter at the intersection of the row and column.
3. Write that letter above the number of the exercise below.

	L	A	Y	A	E	O	T	T	N	S
1	L	A	Y	A	E	O	T	T	N	S
2	R	L	M	E	D	I	W	C	U	A
3	M	O	N	C	T	I	A	G	H	T
5	A	L	J	A	E	L	B	Z	N	O
7	F	C	S	P	F	B	S	D	E	F
9	O	R	W	H	T	Y	S	O	C	N

numerator (row labels) / denominator: 2 3 4 5 6 8 10 16 20 25

Example: Write the percent as a fraction. **1.** 30%

Solution: $\frac{3}{10}$ The letter at the intersection of 3 and 10 is A. Write A above 1.

Write each percent as a fraction or mixed number.

2. $16\frac{2}{3}\%$ _____

3. 12% _____

4. 20% _____

5. $37\frac{1}{2}\%$ _____

6. 35% _____

7. 120% _____

8. 50% _____

9. $83\frac{1}{3}\%$ _____

10. 8% _____

11. 110% _____

12. $12\frac{1}{2}\%$ _____

13. 5% _____

14. 336% _____

15. 90% _____

16. $6\frac{1}{4}\%$ _____

17. 70% _____

18. $166\frac{2}{3}\%$ _____

19. 75% _____

20. $31\frac{1}{4}\%$ _____

21. 15% _____

22. 45% _____

23. $62\frac{1}{2}\%$ _____

24. $87\frac{1}{2}\%$ _____

25. 28% _____

__ __ __ __ __ __ __ __ __   __ __ A __ __ __ __ __ ,
2 18 5 20 4 24 6 11 21   17 16 1 14 3 12 19

__ __ __ __ __ __   __ __ __ __ __
17 9 13 2 22 7   25 10 8 23 15

Percents and Proportions

Writing Percents as Fractions

Percents and Fractions

Certain percents that are equivalent to common fractions are used
so often that it is helpful to memorize them.

**Write each percent as a fraction or a mixed number. Try to
memorize those you do not already know.**

1. 25% _____   2. 50% _____   3. 75% _____   4. 10% _____

5. $33\frac{1}{3}$% _____   6. 40% _____   7. $66\frac{2}{3}$% _____   8. 80% _____

9. 150% _____   10. 120% _____   11. 125% _____   12. 200% _____

13. Match each percent with a fraction pictured below. Write the letter of the pictured
fraction in the blank space above the correct percent. When you have finished, you will
have written the title of the most popular song in the English language.

___ ___ ___ ___ ___

100% 75% $33\frac{1}{3}$% 20% 25%

___ ___ ___ ___ ___ ___ ___ ___

40% 200% 175% 80% 125% $66\frac{2}{3}$% 50% 60%

___ ___   ___ ___ ___

150% $133\frac{1}{3}$% $266\frac{2}{3}$% 300% 250%

Writing Fractions and Mixed Numbers as Percents

Decimals with Fractions

Write $\frac{1}{6}$ as a percent.

$$6\overline{)1.00} \quad 0.16\frac{4}{6}$$

$$\underline{6}$$
$$40$$
$$\underline{36}$$
$$4$$

Divide the numerator of the fraction by the denominator to convert the fraction to a decimal.

Carry out the division to 2 decimal places. Write the remainder as a fraction in lowest terms.

$\frac{1}{6} = 0.16\frac{4}{6} = 0.16\frac{2}{3}$

$0.16\frac{2}{3} = 16\frac{2}{3}\%$

Move the decimal point 2 places to the right and write a percent sign.

Write $8\frac{1}{4}$ as a percent.

$\frac{1}{4} = 0.25$

$8\frac{1}{4} = 8.25$

$8.25 = 825\%$

Move the decimal point 2 places to the right and write a percent sign.

Choose the computation you would use to change each fraction to a percent.

1. $\frac{5}{8}$ a. $5 \div 13$ b. $8 \div 5$ c. $5 \div 8$ _____

2. $\frac{7}{16}$ a. $7 \div 16$ b. $16 \div 7$ c. $7 \div 9$ _____

3. $\frac{7}{9}$ a. $9 \div 7$ b. $7 \div 9$ c. $7 \div 16$ _____

4. $\frac{25}{75}$ a. $25 \div 75$ b. $75 \div 25$ c. $25 \div 100$ _____

Write each fraction or mixed number as a percent.

5. $\frac{3}{10}$ _____   6. $\frac{1}{5}$ _____   7. $\frac{3}{4}$ _____

8. $\frac{7}{8}$ _____   9. $\frac{9}{16}$ _____   10. $\frac{38}{50}$ _____

11. $\frac{9}{24}$ _____   12. $\frac{11}{11}$ _____ 13. $\frac{25}{60}$ _____

14. $\frac{7}{11}$ _____   15. $1\frac{7}{10}$ _____ 16. $6\frac{2}{5}$ _____

Percents and Proportions

Writing Fractions and Mixed Numbers as Percents

In 1886, Samuel Gompers became the first president of an organization of labor unions. By what abbreviation was this organization known?

To solve:

1. Work each exercise.
2. Find each answer in the clue box below and cross out the letter above the answer.
3. Transfer the letters that are not crossed out, in order, to the answer below.

Example: Write the fraction as a percent. 1. $\frac{3}{5}$

Solution: 60%   Cross out the letter Q above 60%.

Write each fraction or mixed number as a percent.

2. $\frac{5}{8}$ _____

3. $\frac{2}{3}$ _____

4. $\frac{83}{100}$ _____

5. $\frac{11}{20}$ _____

6. $\frac{8}{25}$ _____

7. $\frac{60}{300}$ _____

8. $\frac{15}{18}$ _____

9. $\frac{22}{55}$ _____

10. $\frac{4}{25}$ _____

11. $\frac{36}{99}$ _____

12. $\frac{40}{40}$ _____

13. $1\frac{1}{5}$ _____

14. $1\frac{5}{8}$ _____

15. $\frac{5}{4}$ _____

16. $\frac{8}{5}$ _____

17. $\frac{49}{28}$ _____

18. $\frac{10}{9}$ _____

19. $\frac{3}{50}$ _____

20. $3\frac{1}{5}$ _____

21. $\frac{33}{6}$ _____

22. $\frac{3}{30}$ _____

23. $\frac{44}{200}$ _____

A	B	C	D	E	F	G	H	I	J	K	L	M
$37\frac{1}{2}$%	$162\frac{1}{2}$%	83%	6%	$36\frac{4}{11}$%	$133\frac{1}{3}$%	$62\frac{1}{2}$%	120%	$111\frac{1}{9}$%	40%	32%	64%	320%

N	O	P	Ø	R	S	T	U	V	W	X	Y	Z
$83\frac{1}{3}$%	16%	160%	60%	175%	55%	550%	20%	10%	$66\frac{2}{3}$%	125%	100%	22%

— — — — —

NAME _____ CLASS _____ DATE _____

Finding a Percent of a Number

Correct Decimal Form

Find 30% of 700.

30% = 0.3   Write the percent as a decimal.
Move the decimal point 2 places to
the left and drop the percent sign.

$$\begin{array}{r} 700 \\ \times\ 0.3 \\ \hline 210.0 \end{array}$$ Multiply the decimal times the number.

30% of 700 is 210.

Choose the computation you would use to solve the problem.

1. 2% of 195   **a.** 0.2 × 195   **b.** 0.02 × 195   **c.** 2 × 195   _____

2. $5\frac{1}{2}$% of 18   **a.** 0.055 × 18   **b.** $5\frac{1}{2}$ × 18   **c.** 0.55 × 18   _____

3. 0.8% of 7,000   **a.** 0.8 × 7,000   **b.** 0.08 × 7,000   **c.** 0.008 × 7,000   _____

4. 8.4% of 48   **a.** 0.084 × 48   **b.** 8.4 × 48   **c.** 0.84 × 48   _____

Solve.

5. 44% of 82 _____

6. 5% of 187 _____

7. 2% of 3.6 _____

8. 12% of 700 _____

9. 75% of 140 _____

10. 16% of 252 _____

11. 112% of 86 _____

12. 300% of 8.9 _____

13. 1.5% of 50 _____

14. 12.25% of 860 _____

15. 0.1% of 72 _____

16. 9% of 97,000 _____

17. 0.4% of 8,000 _____

18. 2.4% of 2.4 _____

19. 0.08% of 100,000 _____

20. 0.25% of 182 _____

21. $62\frac{1}{2}$% of 576 _____

22. 258% of 12 _____

Percents and Proportions

Finding What Percent One Number Is of Another

45 is what percent of 20?

Think: Is 45 more than 20? Yes. So the fraction needed to solve the problem must be greater than 1.

$\frac{45}{20} > 1; \frac{20}{45} < 1.$

$\frac{45}{20}$ Write a fraction to show what part one number is of the other.

$$\begin{array}{r} 2.25 \\ 20\overline{)45.00} \\ \underline{40} \\ 5\,0 \\ \underline{4\,0} \\ 1\,00 \\ \underline{1\,00} \end{array}$$

Divide the numerator by the denominator. Carry out the division to 2 decimal places.

2.25 = 225%   Move the decimal point 2 places to the right and write a percent sign.

45 is 225% of 20.

Choose whether the fraction to solve the problem is greater than 1 or less than 1.

1. 16 is what percent of 5?   a. greater than 1   b. less than 1 _____

2. What percent of 45 is 18?   a. greater than 1   b. less than 1 _____

3. What percent of 18 is 27?   a. greater than 1   b. less than 1 _____

Choose the correct fraction to show the problem.

4. 50 is what percent of 40?   a. $\frac{50}{40}$ b. $\frac{40}{50}$ c. $\frac{40}{90}$ _____

5. 21 is what percent of 12?   a. $\frac{12}{33}$ b. $\frac{12}{21}$ c. $\frac{21}{12}$ _____

6. What percent of 32 is 76?   a. $\frac{32}{108}$ b. $\frac{32}{76}$ c. $\frac{76}{32}$ _____

7. What percent of 57 is 43?   a. $\frac{57}{43}$ b. $\frac{43}{57}$ c. $\frac{57}{100}$ _____

Solve.

8. 7 is what percent of 10? _____

9. What percent of 40 is 80? _____

10. 36 is what percent of 12? _____

11. 24 is what percent of 48? _____

12. 150 is what percent of 60? _____

13. 20 is what percent of 50? _____

NAME _____ CLASS _____ DATE _____

Finding What Percent One Number Is of Another

Estimating Percents

You can use your estimation skills to find what percent one number is of another.

Example: Use estimation to choose the most reasonable answer from the choices given.

What percent of 800 is 200?   **a.** 250%
What percent of 800 is 2?   **b.** 25%
                              c. 0.25%

Solution: 250% of 800 is $2\frac{1}{2}$ times 800. Therefore, **a** is not a reasonable answer for either question.

25% of 800 would be $\frac{1}{4}$ of 800. Therefore, **b** is a reasonable answer for the first question.

0.25% of 800 would be a very small number. Therefore, **c** is a reasonable answer for the second question.

Choose the most reasonable answer for each question from the choices given. Do not calculate the answers.

1. What percent of 400 is 20? _____   **a.** 50%
                                          b. 5%
   What percent of 400 is 2? _____   **c.** 0.5%

2. What percent of 300 is 33? _____   **a.** 101%
                                          b. 11%
   What percent of 300 is 3? _____   **c.** 1%

3. What percent of 900 is 45? _____   **a.** 500%
                                          b. 50%
   What percent of 90 is 45? _____   **c.** 5%

4. What percent of 1,800 is 720? _____   **a.** 400%
                                          b. 40%
   What percent of 1,800 is 7,200? _____   **c.** 4%

5. What percent of 700 is 3.5? _____   **a.** 5%
                                          b. 0.5%
   What percent of 7,000 is 3.5? _____   **c.** 0.05%

6. What percent of 60 is 1.2? _____   **a.** 20%
                                          b. 2%
   What percent of 600 is 1.2? _____   **c.** 0.2%

NAME ________________ CLASS ________ DATE ________

Percent of Increase or Decrease

Percents and Proportions

Find the percent of increase.

1. 32 to 56 ________

2. 20 to 24 ________

3. 200 to 400 ________

4. 45 to 72 ________

5. $5 to $7 ________

6. $1.00 to $1.25 ________

7. $80 to $88 ________

8. $12.50 to $15.00 ________

9. 180 to 240 ________

10. 32 to 36 ________

11. 14 to 17.5 ________

12. 100 to 250 ________

Find the percent of decrease.

13. 10 to 7 ________

14. 40 to 10 ________

15. 35 to 0 ________

16. 60 to 24 ________

17. 24 to 15 ________

18. 10 to 1 ________

19. 86.25 to 69________

20. 150 to 148.2________

21. $30 to $10 ________

22. $80 to $24 ________

23. $110 to $71.50 ________

24. $97.20 to $85.05 ________

25. Binoculars regularly priced at $84 are on sale for $63. Find the rate of reduction.

____

26. The speed of the world's fastest train increased from 90 miles per hour in 1897 to 150 miles per hour in 1953. Find the percent of increase. ________

27. On October 19, 1987, the Dow Jones average of industrial stock prices fell from 2,247 to 1,739, the largest drop in history. Find the percent of decrease to the nearest tenth.

____

28. The number of whooping cranes known to exist in the wild grew from 15 in 1940 to 90 in 1980. Find the percent of increase. ________

NAME _____ CLASS _____ DATE _____

Finding a Number When a Percent Is Known

Translating Percent Questions

There are three types of percent questions. Each question asks you to find a different number:

6% of 24 is **what number?**
18 is **what percent** of 32?
75 is 3% **of what number?**

To translate these questions into equations, remember that the word *of* always represents multiplication.

Example: 6% of 24 is **what number?**

Solution: $0.06 \times 24 = n$
$1.44 = n$

Example: 18 is **what percent** of 32?

Solution: $18 = n \times 32$
$0.5625 = n$
$n = 56.25\%$

Example: 75 is 3% **of what number?**

Solution: $75 = 0.03 \times n$
$2,500 = n$

Write the equation for each exercise. Then solve.

1. 1% of what number is 68?

2. 2% of 6,250 is what number?

3. 3,000 is what percent of 75,000?

4. 98 is 5% of what number?

5. 10% of what number is 62?

6. 160 is what percent of 800?

7. What number is 25% of 21.6?

8. 69 is what percent of 92?

9. 40% of 375 is what number?

10. 800 is what percent of 320?

11. 125% of 72 is what number?

12. What percent of 316.5 is 37.98?

Percents and Proportions

Finding a Number When a Percent Is Known

In his poem "The Hollow Men," T.S. Eliot made a famous prediction about the end of the world. How did Eliot predict the world would end?

To solve:

1. Work each exercise.
2. In the clue box find the letter that matches each answer.
3. Write that letter above the number of the exercise each time it appears below.

7—M	90—I
16—A	96—W
20—U	120—V
25—S	180—C
27—T	200—O
28—B	250—P
45—E	270—K
51—H	400—G
55—N	500—R

Example: 1. 50% of what number is 8?

Solution: 16   The letter *A* matches 16. Write *A* above 1.

Find the missing numbers.

2. 35% of what number is 70? _____

3. 42 = 600% of what number? _____

4. 63 = 70% of _____

5. $\frac{1}{4}$% of _____ = 0.24

6. $66\frac{2}{3}$% of what number is 34? _____

7. 60 = $62\frac{1}{2}$% of _____

8. 8% of _____ = 2.16

9. 1 is 5% of what number? _____

10. 23% of what number is 6.21? _____

11. 140% of what number is 77? _____

12. 300% of _____ = 81

13. 49 = 175% of _____

14. 36.9 = 82% of _____

15. 0.6% of what number is 3? _____

16. 35 is 8.75% of what number? _____

17. 180% of what number is 99? _____

18. 112 = $44\frac{4}{5}$% of _____

19. $35\frac{5}{8}$% of what number is 9.975? _____

"__ __ __   __ __ __ __   A   __ A __ __
  11 2 10   7 4 8 6   1   19 1 17 16

__ __ __   A   __ __ __ __ __ __ __"
13 9 12   1   5 6 4 3 18 14 15

NAME _____ CLASS _____ DATE _____

Estimation/Mental Math

A weather forcaster announced that on 25% of the Saturdays last summer it rained. Actually, it rained on 3 Saturdays out of 13, or 23.1%. The announcer estimated the percent as follows: $\frac{3}{13} \approx \frac{3}{12}$ and $\frac{3}{12} = \frac{1}{4} = 25\%$.
Therefore, 3 is about 25% of 13.

Example: Estimate 31% of 16.

Solution: 31% ≈ 30%
You can mentally find 30% of a number by multiplying 10% of that number by 3.
30% of 16 = 4.8 (1.6 × 3)
31% of 16 is about 4.8.

Example: Estimate 15% of $15.93.

Solution: You can mentally find 15% of a number by adding 10% of that number to 5% of that number.
Round the dollar amount to a whole number.
$15.93 ≈ $16.00
15% of $16 = (10% of $16) + (5% of $16) = $1.60 + $.80 = $2.40
15% of $15.93 is about $2.40.

Example: 26% of a number is 32. Estimate the number.

Solution: 26% ≈ 25%; 25% = $\frac{1}{4}$
32 ÷ $\frac{1}{4}$ = 32 × 4 = 128
The number is approximately 128.

Estimate.

1. 41% of 120 _____

2. 62% of 55 _____

3. 15% of $63.87 _____

4. 62% of 90 _____

5. 87% of 88 _____

6. 15% of $12.36 _____

7. 102% of 84 _____

8. $18\frac{1}{2}$% of 40 _____

9. 89% of 110 _____

10. 8 is what percent of 42? _____

11. What percent of 40 is 18? _____

12. 3 is what percent of 35? _____

13. What percent of 43.6 is 10.9? _____

14. 83% of what number is 20? _____

15. 78 is 132% of what number? _____

16. 33% of what number is 96? _____

17. 16 is 0.9% of what number? _____

18. 3 is 12% of what number? _____

19. 8 is 16% of what number? _____

20. 7 is 102% of what number? _____

21. 84% of what number is 12? _____

22. In the first round, Ann and her partner scored 29 points. This was 25% of their total. About how many points did they score in the whole match? _____

Proportion

Using Cross Products

Is $\frac{2}{6} = \frac{3}{9}$ a proportion?

Find the cross products.

first   2   3   third   The first and fourth numbers are called the extremes.

second   6   9   fourth   The second and third numbers are called the means.

$2 \times 9 = 18$ product of the extremes
$6 \times 3 = 18$ product of the means

If the product of the extremes is equal to the product of the means, then the statement is a true proportion.
$\frac{2}{6} = \frac{3}{9}$ is a proportion because the product of the extremes is equal to the product of the means.

Are each of the following proportions?

1. $\frac{15}{12} = \frac{5}{4}$ _____

2. $\frac{102}{51} = \frac{1}{2}$ _____

3. $\frac{8}{5} = \frac{176}{110}$ _____

4. $\frac{1}{12} = \frac{12}{144}$ _____

5. $\frac{2}{3} = \frac{4}{9}$ _____

6. $\frac{8}{12} = \frac{5}{8}$ _____

Complete the steps to solve. Then check.

7. $\frac{n}{10} = \frac{5}{2}$

$2 \times n =$ _____

$2n =$ _____

$\frac{2n}{2} =$ _____

$n =$ _____

8. $\frac{n}{6} = \frac{8}{3}$

_____ $= 8 \times 6$

_____ $= 48$

_____ $= \frac{48}{3}$

$n =$ _____

9. $\frac{3}{5} = \frac{12}{n}$

$3 \times n =$ _____

$3n =$ _____

$\frac{3n}{3} =$ _____

$n =$ _____

10. $\frac{9}{6} = \frac{6}{n}$

_____ $= 6 \times 6$

_____ $= 36$

_____ $= \frac{36}{9}$

$n =$ _____

Finding Distances by Using Similar Triangles

Correctly Setting Up Proportions

Find the distance across the swamp if triangles *ABC* and *EDC* are similar.

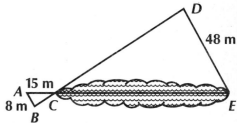

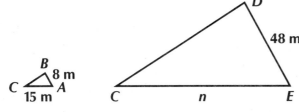

Draw the two triangles next to each other to see the relationships. $\overline{AB}$ corresponds to $\overline{ED}$. $\overline{AC}$ corresponds to $\overline{EC}$.

$$\frac{\text{side } AB}{\text{side } ED} = \frac{\text{side } AC}{\text{side } EC}$$

Let n = the length of side *EC*

$$\frac{8}{48} = \frac{15}{n}$$

$8 \times n = 48 \times 15$ Solve the proportion.

$8n = 720$

$$\frac{8n}{8} = \frac{720}{8}$$

$n = 90$

side *EC* = 90 meters

It is 90 meters across the swamp.

Triangles *JKL* and *MNQ* are similar. Choose the correct answer.

1. Which side of $\triangle JKL$ corresponds to $\overline{NQ}$?

    a. $\overline{LJ}$ **b.** $\overline{JK}$ **c.** $\overline{KL}$ _____

2. Which side of $\triangle MNQ$ corresponds to $\overline{JK}$?

    a. $\overline{NQ}$ **b.** $\overline{MN}$ **c.** $\overline{MQ}$ _____

3. Which proportion can be used to find $\overline{MN}$?

    a. $\dfrac{\overline{MN}}{\overline{JK}} = \dfrac{\overline{MQ}}{\overline{JL}}$ **b.** $\dfrac{\overline{MN}}{\overline{NQ}} = \dfrac{\overline{JL}}{\overline{KL}}$ **c.** $\dfrac{\overline{KL}}{\overline{MN}} = \dfrac{\overline{JL}}{\overline{MQ}}$ _____

4. If $\overline{JL}$ = 6 m, $\overline{KL}$ = 7 m, and $\overline{NQ}$ = 14 m, find $\overline{MQ}$.

    a. 10 m   **b.** 12 m   **c.** 16.3 m   _____

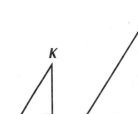

Finding Distances by Using Similar Triangles

On March 30, 1842, the small town of Jefferson, Georgia, was the site of an historic medical achievement by Dr. Crawford Long. What was it?

	0	2	4	6
1	E	N	A	L
3	A	R	T	E
5	H	O	I	M
7	N	G	F	C
9	S	T	S	K

To solve:
1. Work each exercise.
2. Find the first digit of each answer to the left of the clue box. Find the second digit above the clue box. Find the letter at the intersection of the row and column.
3. Write that letter above the number of the exercise each time it appears below.

Example: 1. Triangles *GHI* and *JKL* are similar. How long is $\overline{KL}$?

Solution: 30 cm   The letter at the intersection of 3 and 0 is *A*. Write *A* above 1.

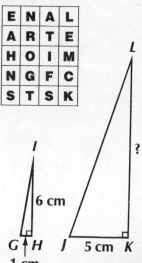

Triangles *ABC* and *DEF* are similar. Find the indicated missing lengths.

	$\overline{AB}$	$\overline{BC}$	$\overline{AC}$	$\overline{DE}$	$\overline{EF}$	$\overline{DF}$
2.	2 cm	3 cm		36 m	___ m	
3.	15 in.		19 in.	60 yd		___ yd
4.		1 ft	2 ft		47 mi	___ mi
5.	40 cm	___ cm		48 m	60 m	

Triangles *MNO* and *QPO* are similar. Find the indicated missing lengths.

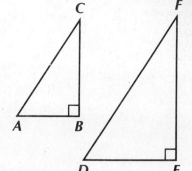

	$\overline{MN}$	$\overline{NO}$	$\overline{MO}$	$\overline{PQ}$	$\overline{OP}$	$\overline{OQ}$
6.	21 in.		14 in.	18 in.		___ in.
7.		51 mm	30 mm		___ mm	20 mm
8.		20 m	___ m		5 m	9 m

FIRST USE OF   <u>A</u> __ __ __ __ __ __ __ __ __
                  1   6 8 4 7 5 8 7 2 3

Customary Measures of Length

Renaming in Computations

Add 3 yards 2 feet and 5 yards 2 feet.

$\begin{array}{ll} \quad 3 \text{ yd } 2 \text{ ft} & \text{First, add feet.} \\ + \; 5 \text{ yd } 2 \text{ ft} & \text{Then add yards.} \\ \quad 8 \text{ yd } 4 \text{ ft} \end{array}$

Since 4 feet is more than 1 yard (3 ft = 1 yd), rename.

4 ft = 3 ft + 1 ft = 1 yd + 1 ft
8 yd 4 ft = 8 yd + 1 yd + 1 ft = 9 yd 1 ft

Divide 9 yards 2 feet 10 inches by 2.

$\begin{array}{l} \quad\;\; \underline{4 \text{ yd}} \\ 2)\overline{9 \text{ yd } 2 \text{ ft } 10 \text{ in.}} \qquad \text{Divide: } 9 \div 2 = 4 \text{ R1} \\ \quad\;\; \underline{8 \text{ yd}} \\ \quad\;\; 1 \text{ yd} \qquad\qquad\qquad \text{Rename 1 yard as 3 feet.} \end{array}$

$\begin{array}{l} \quad\;\; \underline{4 \text{ yd } 2 \text{ ft}} \\ 2)\overline{9 \text{ yd } \overset{5}{2} \text{ ft } 10 \text{ in.}} \qquad 3 \text{ feet} + 2 \text{ feet} = 5 \text{ feet} \\ \quad\;\; \underline{8 \text{ yd } 4 \text{ ft}} \qquad\quad \text{Divide: } 5 \div 2 = 2 \text{ R1} \\ \quad\;\; \cancel{1 \text{ yd}} \; 1 \text{ ft} \qquad\quad \text{Rename 1 foot as 12 inches.} \end{array}$

$\begin{array}{l} \quad\;\; \underline{4 \text{ yd } 2 \text{ ft } 11 \text{ in.}} \\ 2)\overline{9 \text{ yd } \overset{5}{2} \text{ ft } \overset{22}{10} \text{ in.}} \qquad 12 \text{ inches} + 10 \text{ inches} = 22 \text{ inches} \\ \quad\quad\; \underline{4 \text{ ft}} \qquad\qquad\quad \text{Divide: } 22 \div 2 = 11 \\ \quad\quad\; \cancel{1 \text{ ft}} \end{array}$

Solve.

1. 8 ft 7 in.
     + 9 ft 11 in.

2. 10 yd 3 in.
     + 4 yd 10 in.

3. 14 yd 1 ft
     − 6 yd 2 ft

4. 8 yd 7 in.
     − 3 yd 9 in.

5. 6 yd 2 ft
          × 3

6. 3 yd 2 ft 4 in.
              × 4

7. 3)$\overline{16 \text{ yd } 2 \text{ ft } 3 \text{ in.}}$

8. 2)$\overline{13 \text{ yd } 4 \text{ in.}}$

Measurement

Customary Measures of Length

The name of which South American country comes from the Inca word meaning "where the land ends"?

To solve:

1. Work each exercise.
2. Transfer digits as indicated by arrows.
3. Match each number in the row of boxes below with a letter of the alphabet. Write the letter below the box.

Complete.

1. 6 ft = ☐☐ in.

4. 144 in. = __☐ ft

2. ☐ yd = __☐__ in.

5. ☐5 yd = ☐__ ft

3. ☐ ft 9 in. = __☐ in.

6. ☐ yd 48 in. = __☐ ft

7.   2 ft 1 1 in.
      + 3 ft   9 in.
      ─────────────
        __ ft ☐ in.

8.   1 yd 18 in.
          ×   8
          ─────────────
           ☐☐ yd

9.   1 8 yd   3 in.
      − 1 4 yd 2 ft 7 in.
      ─────────────────
        ☐ yd   __ in.

— — — — — —

A	B	C	D	E	F	G	H	I	J	K	L	M	N	O	P	Q	R	S	T	U	V	W	X	Y	Z
1	2	3	4	5	6	7	8	9	10	11	12	13	14	15	16	17	18	19	20	21	22	23	24	25	26

Measurement

Customary Measures of Weight

The god of shepherds and hunters in Greek mythology was portrayed as an odd-looking man with the horns, legs, and ears of a goat. He played beautiful music on a reed flute. Name him.

To solve:

1. Work each exercise.
2. Find the digits of each answer on the correct number line. Cross out the letter over each digit. Some letters may be crossed out more than once.
3. Transfer the letters that are not crossed out, in order, to the answer below.

Example: **1.** 3 lb = ___ oz

Solution: 48   On number line I, cross out the letters over 4 and 8.

Complete.

2. 7 lb 12 oz = _____ oz

3. $6\frac{1}{2}$ l. ton = _____ lb

4. 17 T 1,800 lb = _____ lb

5. 304 oz = _____ lb

Exercises 1–5

I.

6. 498,000 lb = _____ T

7. 316,000 lb = _____ T

8. 720,000 lb = _____ T

Exercises 6–8

II.

9. 10 oz = _____ lb

10. 1,700 lb = _____ T

11. 375 lb = _____ T

12. 1,680 lb = _____ l. ton

Exercises 9–12

III.

___ ___ ___
line line line
  I   II   III

Customary Liquid Measures

Renaming in Computations

Multiply 8 gallons 1 quart by 6.

8 gal 1 qt	First, multiply 6 × 1 quart.
× 6	Then multiply 6 × 8 gallons.
48 gal 6 qt	

Since 6 quarts is more than 1 gallon (4 qt = 1 gal), rename.

6 qt = 4 qt + 2 qt = 1 gal + 2 qt

48 gal 6 qt = 48 gal + 1 gal + 2 qt = 49 gal 2 qt

Complete each sentence.

1. To change ounces to quarts, you _____ by _____.
   (multiply/divide)

2. To change gallons to ounces, you _____ by _____.
   (multiply/divide)

3. To change pints to quarts, you _____ by _____.
   (multiply/divide)

4. To change pints to ounces, you _____ by _____.
   (multiply/divide)

Solve.

5. 2 gal 3 qt
   + 4 gal 2 qt

6. 3 qt 1 pt 10 oz
   + 7 qt 1 pt 14 oz

7. 4 pt 1 oz
   − 1 pt 9 oz

8. 6 gal 1 qt
   − 2 gal 3 qt

9. 13 qt 1 pt
        × 4

10. 1 pt 9 oz
         × 3

11. 7)15 qt 10 oz

12. 3)10 gal 3 qt 1 oz

Customary Liquid Measures

The world's longest glacier was discovered in 1956 in the Australian Antarctic Territory. What is the name of this 250-mile river of ice?

To solve:
1. Work each exercise.
2. Find each answer below and write the letter of the exercise above the answer.

Example: E. 2 pt = ___ oz

Solution: 32   Write *E* above 32.

Complete.

A. $7\frac{1}{2}$ pt = _____ oz	**B.** $1\frac{3}{4}$ qt = _____ oz	**A.** $3\frac{1}{4}$ gal = _____ oz
I. 2 qt 7 oz = _____ oz	**E.** $8\frac{1}{2}$ qt = _____ pt	**A.** 20 gal = _____ pt
C. 3 qt 2 pt = _____ pt	**I.** 80 oz = _____ pt	**R.** $11\frac{1}{4}$ gal = _____ qt
S. 8 gal 3 qt = _____ qt	**E.** 52 pt = _____ qt	**T.** 224 oz = _____ qt
H. 216 qt = _____ gal	**S.** 184 pt = _____ gal	**P.** 768 oz = _____ gal
G. 2 oz = _____ pt	**R.** $\frac{3}{4}$ pt = _____ qt	**M.** 80 oz = _____ gal

Solve. Express each answer in quarts.

E.   7 qt 10 oz
      5 qt 13 oz
   + 3 qt 9 oz

L.   19 qt 1 pt
      − 4 qt 3 pt

F.   4 qt 8 oz
      ×   8

S. 5)13 gal 3 qt

							-						E	
14	160	$\frac{5}{8}$	56	16	45	7		34	71	11	54	32		$\frac{3}{8}$

5	8	17		6	120	23	35	416	$\frac{1}{8}$	26

Measuring Time

Use of Conversion Factors

Change 10 years to days.

First, determine the number of leap years in 10 years. Divide 10 by 4, since every fourth year is a leap year. Disregard the fractional part of your answer.

$$10 \div 4 = 2\frac{1}{2} \rightarrow 2$$

There are 2 leap years in a period of 10 years.

1 year = 365 days
1 leap year = 366 days

(2 × 366) + (8 × 365)   Multiply 366 by 2.
   732 + 2,920   Multiply 365 by the remaining 8 years.
    3,652 days   Add the products.

There are 3,652 days in 10 years.

Complete each sentence.

1. When changing several years to days, use _____ days for every fourth year to account for leap year.

2. There are _____ days in 5 years.

3. There are 2,556 days in _____ years.

Complete.

4. $3\frac{1}{2}$ h = _____ min

5. 360 h = _____ da

6. 9 yr = _____ da

7. 2 da 8 h = _____ h

8. 180 mo = _____ yr

9. $1\frac{1}{2}$ yr = _____ mo

Solve.

10.   12 h 37 min
    + 8 h 25 min

11.   3 min 7 s
    − 2 min 28 s

12.   8 yr 3 mo
        × 9

13. 4)5 wk 5 da

Measurement

Measuring Time

In 1939, Igor Sikorsky built the first practical helicopter. What did he say about individual achievement?

To solve:
1. Work each exercise.
2. In the clue box find the word that matches each answer.
3. Write that word above the number of the exercise below.

Example: **1.** 3 min = _____ s

Solution: 180 The word *the* matches 180.
Write *the* above 1.

Complete.

2. 1,080 s = _____ min

3. 9 da 17 h = _____ h

4. 936 h = _____ da

5. $13\frac{1}{3}$ yr = _____ mo

6. $10\frac{1}{2}$ yr = _____ wk

7. 988 wk = _____ yr

8. 25 s = _____ min

9. 20 min = _____ h

10. 4 h = _____ da

11. 219 da = _____ yr

12. Find the number of minutes from 9:47 A.M. to 1:33 P.M. the same day. _____

Clue box
$\frac{1}{3}$—that
$\frac{1}{6}$—remains
$\frac{3}{5}$—the
$\frac{5}{12}$—mankind
18—spark
19—of
39—ahead
160—still
180—the
226—individual
233—work
546—moves

Measurement

" _____ _____ _____ THE____ _____
    11   3   7   1   12

_____ _____ THE____ _____ _____
    5   10   1   2   9

_____ _____ _____."
    6   8   4

Perimeter of a Rectangle

Find the perimeter of a rectangle
18 feet long and 13 feet wide.

13 ft

18 ft

Remember, the formula for finding the perimeter of a rectangle
is $P = 2(l + w)$ where P = perimeter, l = length, and w = width.

$P = 2(l + w)$
$P = 2(18 + 13)$ Substitute the given length and width in the formula.
$P = 2(31)$ First, add within the parentheses.
$P = 62$ Then multiply.

The perimeter is 62 feet.

Choose the correct answer.

1. Find the perimeter of a rectangle with a width of 82 millimeters and a length of 106
   millimeters.

   a. $3(82 + 106)$ **b.** $2(82 + 106)$ **c.** $2 \times 82 \times 106$ _____

2. Find the perimeter of a rectangle with a width of $4\frac{1}{2}$ inches and a length of $5\frac{11}{16}$ inches.

   a. $2(4\frac{1}{2} + 5\frac{11}{16})$ **b.** $2 + 4\frac{1}{2} + 5\frac{11}{16}$ **c.** $2 \times 4\frac{1}{2} \times 5\frac{11}{16}$ _____

Find the perimeter of each rectangle with the given dimensions.

3. $l = 4.5$ m   4. $l = 3\frac{3}{8}$ in.   5. $l = 4$ ft 8 in.
   $w = 2.7$ m $w = 1\frac{3}{16}$ in. $w = 2$ ft 7 in.

_____   _____   _____

Solve.

6. What is the perimeter of a rectangle if its length is 58 centimeters and its width is 42

   centimeters? _____

7. How many yards of fencing are required to fence a corral 100 yards by 96 yards?

_____

Measurement

Perimeter of a Rectangle

The French Revolution began on June 20, 1789, when the delegates to the Third Estate vowed not to disband until King Louis XVI granted France a Constitution. What was the unusual setting for this solemn oath?

To solve:

1. Work each exercise.
2. In the clue box find the letter that matches each answer.
3. Write that letter above the number of the exercise below.

6 yd—L	$120—B
10 in.—E	144 in.—W
10.18 km—I	159 ft—H
$14\frac{1}{8}$ in.—N	287 m—U
19 ft—N	$318—T
21 m—C	368 mm—R
28 ft—S	$370—A
36 ft—I	398 mm—O
$106—M	$450—N

Example: **1.** What is the perimeter of a rectangle measuring 3 inches by 2 inches?

Solution: 10 in.   The letter E matches 10 inches. Write E above 1.

Find the perimeter of each rectangle.

2. l = 3.24 km
w = 1.85 km

3. l = 119 mm
w = 65 mm

4. l = 88.38 m
w = 55.12 m

5. $l = 4\frac{3}{4}$ in.
$w = 2\frac{5}{16}$ in.

_____   _____   _____   _____

6. What is the perimeter of a rectangle if its length is 123 millimeters and its width is 76 millimeters? __ _____

7. A fence costing $3 per foot is to be built around a yard 32 feet long by 21 feet wide. How much will the fence cost? _____

8. How many feet of molding are needed to construct a rectangular frame 64 inches by 104 inches? _____

9. How many meters of decorative border are needed to drape a rectangular bandstand 632 centimeters by 418 centimeters? _____

A   __ __E__ __ __ __ __   __ __ __ __ __
     7   1   5   5   2   8   9   6   4   3   7

Measurement

Area of a Rectangle

Franklin D. Roosevelt is the only person to have served four
terms as President of the United States. He defeated
Thomas E. Dewey in 1944. Name the other three
opponents he defeated.

To solve:

1. Work each exercise.
2. Find the first digit of each answer to the left of the answer box.
   Find the second and third digits above the answer box.
3. Write the letter of the exercise in the box at the intersection of
   the row and column.

Example: **W.** Find the area of a rectangle 30 centimeters long and 20
centimeters wide.

Solution: 600 cm²   Write *W* at the intersection of 6 and 00.

Find the area of each rectangle with the given measurements.

L. l = 25 m; w = 12 m; _____

D. l = 8.65 cm; w = 4 cm; _____

A. l = 19.5 km; w = 16 km; _____

K. l = 35 cm; w = 19 cm; _____

L. l = 42.2 ft; w = 15 ft; _____

H. l = 15 yd; w = 6 yd 2 ft; _____

O. l = 0.8 km; w = 0.14 km; _____

V. l = 20 m; w = 7.3 m; _____

E. l = 34 yd; w = 20 yd 18 in.; _____

O. l = 19 ft; w = 7 ft; _____

I. l = 30 mm; w = 22.9 mm; _____

E. l = 1.5 yd; w = 1.1 yd; _____

N. l = 9 in.; w = 4.3 in.; _____

O. l = 10 ft; w = 36 ft 6 in.; _____

N. l = 18 ft 6 in.; w = 18 ft; _____

L. l = 3.4 cm; w = 1.9 cm; _____

I. l = 51 in.; w = 12 in.; _____

R. l = 1 cm 7 mm; w = 1 cm 1 mm;

_____

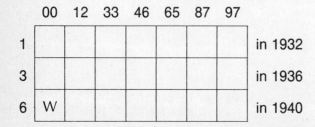

	00	12	33	46	65	87	97	
1								in 1932
3								in 1936
6	W							in 1940

Area of a Square

Square Units

Find the area of a square whose
side is 4 feet long.

4 ft

4 ft

The formula for finding the area of a square is $A = s^2$
where A = area and s = length of a side.

$A = s^2$
$A = 4^2$ Substitute the length of the side for s in the formula.
$A = 16$ ft^2 Remember, feet × feet = square feet.

$A = 16$ ft^2 Check your answer by counting the square
             units in the picture.

The area of the square is 16 square feet.

Choose the correct area of a square with the given side.

1. 8.2 cm   **a.** 8.2   **b.** $(8.2)^2$ **c.** 8.2 × 2   _____

2. 12 ft   **a.** $(12)^2$ **b.** 12 × 2   **c.** 12   _____

3. 3 ft 1 in.   **a.** $2 \times 3\frac{1}{12}$ **b.** $(3\frac{1}{2})^2$ **c.** $(37)^2$ _____

4. 2 yd 1 ft   **a.** 49 yd^2 **b.** 49 ft^2 **c.** 16 yd 1 ft   _____

5. $1\frac{1}{2}$ ft   **a.** 324 ft^2 **b.** 324 in.   **c.** 324 in.^{2} _____

Find the area of each square with the given side measurement.

6. 13 m _____   **7.** 2.5 cm _____

8. 4 yd _____   **9.** 12.6 mm _____

10. $5\frac{2}{3}$ ft _____   **11.** $7\frac{1}{2}$ in. _____

12. 14 m _____   **13.** 1 mi _____

Measurement

Circumference of a Circle

Name the American composer who wrote some of the most exciting and innovating music of the twentieth century while simultaneously pursuing a career as an insurance executive.

To solve:
1. Work each exercise.
2. Find the digits of each answer on the corresponding number line. Cross out the letter that matches each digit. Some letters may be crossed out more than once.
3. Transfer the letters that are not crossed out, in order, to the answer below.

Example: **1.** Find the diameter of a circle with radius 3 meters.

Solution: 6 m   On number line I, cross out the letter *L*.

Find the diameter of a circle with the given radius.

2. 28 in.   **3.** 123.5 m   **4.** 41.25 mm

_____   _____   _____

Find the radius of a circle with the given diameter.

5. 41 yd   **6.** 103.28 km   **7.** 1,526 ft

_____   _____   _____

Exercises 1–7

R T N A P S L O G I
I. ◄─┼─┼─┼─┼─┼─┼─┼─┼─┼─►
   0 1 2 3 4 5 6 7 8 9

Use $\pi = 3.14$ to find the circumference of a circle with the given dimensions.

8. $d = 49$ m   **9.** $r = 70$ yd   **10.** $d = 65$ mi

_____   _____   _____

Exercises 8–10

W A N T E C O V M R
II. ◄─┼─┼─┼─┼─┼─┼─┼─┼─┼─►
   0 1 2 3 4 5 6 7 8 9

Use $\pi = 3.14$ to find the diameter of a circle with the given circumference.

11. 124.03 cm   **12.** 659.4 m   **13.** 274.436 ft

_____   _____   _____

Exercises 11–13

N H C S B R E A T F
III. ◄─┼─┼─┼─┼─┼─┼─┼─┼─┼─►
   0 1 2 3 4 5 6 7 8 9

Use $\pi = 3.14$ to find the radius of a circle with the given circumference.

14. 1,067.6 m   **15.** 185.26 cm   **16.** 2,939.04 mm

_____   _____   _____

Exercises 14–16

E T P S R A D N L W
IV. ◄─┼─┼─┼─┼─┼─┼─┼─┼─┼─►
   0 1 2 3 4 5 6 7 8 9

CHARLES   ____ ____ ____ ____
          line line line line
           I   II   III   IV

Measurement

Area of a Circle

Choose the Correct Formula

Find the area of a circle with a diameter of 7 meters.

Finding the area of a circle is not the same as finding the circumference of a circle. Different formulas are used.

$$C = \pi d \qquad A = \frac{1}{4}\pi d^2$$
$$C = 2\pi r \qquad A = \pi r^2$$

Choose the correct formula.

To find the area of a circle, choose either $A = \frac{1}{4}\pi d^2$ or $A = \pi r^2$.

Since the diameter is given, use $A = \frac{1}{4}\pi d^2$.

Remember $\pi = 3.14$.

$A = \frac{1}{4} \times 3.14 \times 7^2$ Substitute the values for π and the diameter.

$A = \frac{1}{4} \times 3.14 \times 49$ First, square the diameter.

$A = \frac{153.86}{4}$ Now multiply.

$A = 38.465 \text{ m}^2$ Then divide by 4.

The area of the circle is 38.465 square meters.

Choose the correct formula.

1. Find the area of a circle whose diameter is $3\frac{1}{2}$ inches.

    a. $C = \pi d$ **b.** $A = \pi r^2$ **c.** $A = \frac{1}{4}\pi d^2$ _____

2. Find the area of a circle whose radius is 13 meters.

    a. $C = 2\pi r$ **b.** $A = \pi r^2$ **c.** $A = \frac{1}{4}\pi d^2$ _____

Find the area of each circle with the given dimensions.

3. $d = 5$ ft _____

4. $r = 26$ cm _____

5. $d = 4.2$ m _____

6. $r = 0.3$ mm _____

7. $d = 5$ ft 1 in. _____

8. $r = \frac{1}{5}$ mi _____

9. A dog is running on a 14-foot leash held down at one end. What area can the

    dog cover? _____

Measurement

Customary Measures of Area

Use of Conversion Factors

Change 9,680 square yards to acres.

Remember: 1 acre = 4,840 yd²

$9{,}680 \text{ yd}^2 \times \dfrac{1 \text{ acre}}{4{,}840 \text{ yd}^2} = \dfrac{9{,}680}{4{,}840} = 2$ acres

An acre is a square unit. Do not write *acres²*.

Change 2.5 square feet to square inches.

Remember: 1 ft² = 144 in.²

$2.5 \text{ ft}^2 \times \dfrac{144 \text{ in.}^2}{1 \text{ ft}^2} = 2.5 \times 144 = 360 \text{ in.}^2$

Complete each sentence.

1. To change square yards to square feet, you _____ by _____.
(multiply/divide)

2. To change acres to square miles, you _____ by _____.
(multiply/divide)

Choose the correct answer.

3. 9 ft² = ___ yd²   **a.** 3   **b.** 9   **c.** 1   _____

4. 1,280 acres = ___ mi²   **a.** 4   **b.** 2   **c.** 1   _____

5. 1 ft² = ___ in.²   **a.** 64   **b.** 144   **c.** 200   _____

6. 1,296 in.² = ___ yd²   **a.** 1   **b.** 2   **c.** 3   _____

Complete.

7. 8 ft² = _____ in.²

8. 2 yd² = _____ in.²

9. 4.8 mi² = _____ acres

10. 75 yd² = _____ ft²

11. 2,080 acres = _____ mi²

12. 81 ft² = _____ yd²

13. What part of a square foot is 72 square inches? ___

14. What part of a square yard is 3 square feet? ___

Customary Measures of Volume

Use of Conversion Factors

Change 54 cubic feet to cubic yards.

Remember: $1 \text{ yd}^3 = 27 \text{ ft}^3$

Since a cubic yard is a larger unit than a cubic foot, divide by the conversion factor.

$54 \text{ ft}^3 \times \dfrac{1 \text{ yd}^3}{27 \text{ ft}^3} = \dfrac{54}{27} = 2 \text{ yd}^3$

Change 2.3 cubic feet to cubic inches.

Remember: $1 \text{ ft}^3 = 1{,}728 \text{ in.}^3$

Since a cubic inch is a smaller unit than a cubic foot, multiply by the conversion factor.

$2.3 \text{ ft}^3 \times \dfrac{1{,}728 \text{ in.}^3}{1 \text{ ft}^3} = 2.3 \times 1{,}728 = 3{,}974.4 \text{ in.}^3$

Complete each sentence.

1. To change cubic feet to cubic yards, you _____ by _____.
   (multiply/divide)

2. To change cubic feet to cubic inches, you _____ by _____..
   (multiply/divide)

3. To change cubic yards to cubic inches, you _____ by _____.
   (multiply/divide)

4. To change cubic inches to cubic feet, you _____ by _____.
   (multiply/divide)

Complete.

5. $8.4 \text{ yd}^3 =$ _____ ft^3

6. $3.6 \text{ ft}^3 =$ _____ in.^3

7. $864 \text{ in.}^3 =$ _____ ft^3

8. $69{,}984 \text{ in.}^3 =$ _____ yd^3

9. $171 \text{ ft}^3 =$ _____ yd^3

10. $5{,}875.2 \text{ in.}^3 =$ _____ ft^3

11. $5 \text{ yd}^3 =$ _____ in.^3

12. $2.1 \text{ yd}^3 =$ _____ in.^3

13. What part of a cubic foot is 288 in.^3? ___

14. What part of a cubic yard is 24 ft^3? ___

Customary Measures of Volume

Landscaping

Before ordering topsoil, a landscaper figures out how much ground the topsoil must cover and how deep it must be. One cubic foot measures 1 foot by 1 foot by 1 foot (or 12 inches by 12 inches by 12 inches). Therefore, one cubic foot of topsoil would cover an area that is 12 inches long, 12 inches wide, and 12 inches deep.

Example: Jack Strout wants to spread one cubic foot of topsoil so that it is 4 inches deep instead of 12 inches deep. How many square inches can he cover?

Solution: Picture the cubic foot of topsoil sliced into 1-inch layers as shown in the diagram at the right. Each layer is 1 foot long, 1 foot wide, and 1 inch deep.

Find how many 4-inch deep layers there are in the cubic foot of the topsoil.

$12 \div 4 = 3$

There are three 4-inch layers.

Imagine placing those three 4-inch layers side by side. Each layer would cover a 12-inch by 12-inch area.

$3 \times (12 \text{ in.} \times 12 \text{ in.}) = 432 \text{ in.}^2$

The three 4-inch layers would cover 432 square inches.

Find how many square inches 1 cubic foot of topsoil will cover when spread to each depth listed below.

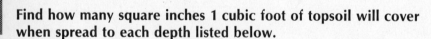

1. 2 in. _____
2. 3 in. _____
3. 6 in. _____
4. $1\frac{1}{2}$ in. _____
5. 5 in. _____
6. 10 in. _____

Solve.

7. A cubic yard of topsoil is 1 yard long, 1 yard wide, and 1 yard deep. How many square feet can 1 cubic yard cover when it is spread $1\frac{1}{2}$ feet deep? _____

Estimation/Mental Math

A shovel is about 1 meter (m) long. The head of a thumbtack is about 1 centimeter (cm) wide. The point of a thumbtack is about 1 millimeter (mm) wide. The landing strip of a small airport is about 1 kilometer (km) long.

The mass of a hammer is about 1 kilogram (kg). The mass of a nail is about 1 gram (g). The mass of a piece of sawdust is about 1 milligram (mg).

A can of motor oil contains 1 liter (L). The spill of a drop of oil is about 1 milliliter (mL).

Circle the appropriate measure.

1. mass of a screwdriver   46 mg   46 g   46 kg
2. mass of a tennis racket   5 g   50 g   500 g
3. mass of a baby   75 g   7.5 kg   0.75 kg
4. mass of a dictionary   0.2 kg   2 kg   20 kg
5. mass of a grain of sand   1 mg   1 g   1 kg
6. paint can   4 L   4 mL
7. drinking glass   250 L   250 mL
8. bathtub   400 mL   400 L
9. soup spoon   1.5 mL   15 mL
10. length of a roadrace   6 m   6 km

Which metric unit of length makes the statement reasonable? Write kilometer, meter, centimeter, or millimeter.

11. A pen is about 14 _____ long.
12. A pencil point is about 1 _____ wide.
13. A coffee mug is about 90 _____ tall.
14. An ear of corn is about 20 _____ long.
15. Two cities could be 12 _____ apart.
16. Motion picture film is 35 _____ wide.
17. A discus is thrown 56 _____.
18. A person can jump 1.5 _____ high.
19. A pilot flew 5,000 _____ yesterday.
20. A newborn baby is about 50 _____ long.

Estimation/Mental Math

Customary Units of Length

1 foot (ft) = 12 inches (in.)
1 yard (yd) = 3 feet (ft) or 36 inches (in.)
1 mile (mi) = 5,280 feet (ft)

Customary Units of Weight

1 pound (lb) = 16 ounces (oz)
1 ton (T) = 2,000 pounds (lb)

Customary Units of Capacity

1 quart (qt) = 2 pints (pt)
1 gallon (gal) = 4 quarts (qt)

Complete.

1. 3 T = _____ lb

2. 80 oz = _____ lb

3. 4 oz = _____ lb

4. 3 T = _____ oz

5. 72 in. = _____ yd

6. 2 mi = _____ yd

7. 8,500 lb = _____ T

8. 18 in. = _____ yd

9. 8 yd = _____ ft

10. 30 in. = _____ yd

11. 8 qt = _____ pt

12. 56 pt = _____ gal

13. $6\frac{1}{2}$ gal = _____ qt

14. 104 pt = _____ gal

Add, subtract, multiply, or divide mentally.

15.   9 ft 26 in.
    + 17 ft 10 in.

16.   25 lb 18 oz
    + 44 lb 6 oz

17.   7 gal 2 qt
    − 2 gal 3 qt

18.   7 yd 1 ft
    − 3 yd 2 ft

19.   4 qt 1 pt
    ×   4

20.   3 lb 8 oz
    ×   4

21. 3)11 lb 4 oz

22. 9)10 T 700 lb

23. 7)23 lb 3 oz

24.   5 h 16 min
    ×   5

25.   3 h 30 min
    ×   6

26. 3)2 da 15 h 27 min

27. Mary Alice had three prize pumpkins for the county fair. The pumpkins weighed 11 pounds 11 ounces, 15 pounds 3 ounces, and 6 pounds 2 ounces. What was the total weight of the three pumpkins? _____ What was the average weight? _____

28. If 1 quart of milk costs $.49, what is the cost of 3 quarts? _____

Measurement

Calculator

Use a calculator to add, subtract, multiply, or divide.

1. 65.014 g + 17.26 g + 100.79 g + 194 g + 6.852 g _____

2. 237.068 kg − 42.615 kg _____

3. 51.627 km × 23 _____

4. 64,828.4 L ÷ 182 _____

5. 610,217 m + 57.89 m + 152,086.7 m _____

6. 1,895.57 g − 1,604.81 g _____

7. 0.7814 m × 62 _____

8. 474.5763 cm ÷ 0.87 _____

9. 153.27 mL + 0.683 mL + 5.479 mL + 16.3 mL _____

10. 7.8952 mg − 0.91376 mg _____

11. 0.609 cm × 1.4 _____

12. 168.0536 L ÷ 5.72 _____

Solve.

13. A laboratory technician analyzed 82 samples. Each sample weighed 75 mg. Find the total

weight of the samples. _____

14. An empty sample vial weighs 2.864 g. The vial with the sample in it weighs 11.032 g. Find

the weight of the sample. _____

15. A laboratory technician wants to prepare 100 mL of a mixture of solution A and solution B.
He starts with 27.82 mL of solution A. How much of solution B should he add?

_____

16. If each unit under a microscope represents 3.56 mm, how long is a leaf that measures 6.5

units under the microscope? _____

17. A solution is to be 6.5% sodium hydroxide by weight. How much sodium hydroxide is

needed for 245 g of solution? _____

18. A laboratory technician combined 45.36 g of sample A, 16.063 g of sample B, and 0.1857 g

of sample C. Find the combined weight of the sample. _____

Bar Graphs

Using Pictographs

Sometimes pictographs are used to present data. In a pictograph, a symbol is used to represent a specific number of objects or persons.

Example: The symbol at the right represents 2 million television viewers. How many symbols represent 7 million viewers?

☐ = 2 million viewers

Solution: $\dfrac{7 \text{ million}}{2 \text{ million}} = 3\frac{1}{2}$

$3\frac{1}{2}$ symbols represent 7 million viewers.

☐ ☐ ☐ ⊏

Determine how many symbols are needed to represent the following television audiences if one symbol represents 2 million viewers.

1. 8 million _____

2. 3 million _____

3. 15 million _____

4. 2.5 million _____

Use the pictograph below to find how many viewers watch each show.

Soap Opera Audiences

Quiz Mania	☐	☐	☐	☐
Mystery Theatre	☐	☐	⊏	
The Music Hour	☐	☐	☐	☐ ⊏
Memorial Hospital	☐	☐	☐	⊏

☐ = 2 million viewers

5. Quiz Mania _____

6. Mystery Theatre _____

7. The Music Hour _____

8. Memorial Hospital _____

On a separate sheet of paper, make a pictograph using the data below. Use 1 antenna to represent 10 million homes.

9. 80.1 million homes have color television sets.

7.7 million homes have black and white television sets only.

36.9 million homes have only one television set.

48.7 million homes have more than one television set.

Bar Graphs

Choosing Scales

Construct a bar graph from the following test scores:
Test 1, 82; Test 2, 78; Test 3, 93; Test 4, 81; Test 5, 85.

Choose a vertical scale.

If the scale is by ones, the graph will be too large.
If it is by 20s, the columns will all be about the same height.
Try a scale of 10. Mark the scale on the vertical axis. Record
each test number on the horizontal axis.

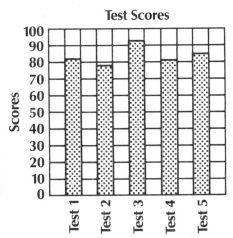

Draw a bar to represent Test 1.
It should extend slightly above 80.
Draw a bar to represent Test 2.
It should end just below 80.
Continue with the other test scores.

Choose the best scale for the data given.

1. Numbers of bus riders over a 4-month period:
   Jan., 42,000; Feb., 38,000; Mar., 52,000; Apr., 46,000
   a. by 100s   **b.** by 1,000s   **c.** by 5,000s _____

2. Average rainfall amounts in different locations:
   Porter, 12 in.; Alanville, 18 in.; Carter, 29 in.; Hughes, 14 in.; Brown City, 23 in.
   a. by $\frac{1}{4}$ in.   **b.** by 3 in.   **c.** by 10 in. _____

3. Make a bar graph for exercise 1.   4. Make a bar graph for exercise 2.

Data Analysis

Broken-Line Graphs

Choosing Scales

Construct a broken-line graph showing the temperatures in St. James on January 12: 2 A.M., 22°; 6 A.M., 18°; 10 A.M., 24°; 2 P.M., 28°; 6 P.M., 25°; 10 P.M., 24°.

Choose a vertical scale. Since the range of data is not too large—10°—you could mark every degree or every 2 degrees. Mark the scale on the vertical axis. Note the jagged line at the bottom of the vertical axis. This indicates that the numbers between 0 and 18 are not included.
Mark the time along the horizontal axis.

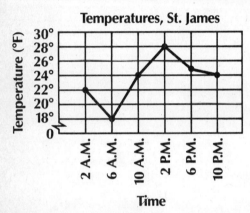

Find 2 A.M. on the horizontal axis.
Move up the graph until you come to 22°.
Mark a dot on the graph.
Do the same with each time and temperature.
Join the dots with line segments.

Choose the best scale for the data given.

1. Sales for 6 months at the Card Shop are Jan., $3,000; Feb., $2,800; Mar., $3,400; Apr., $2,900; May, $3,100; June, $3,300.
   a. each $10   **b.** each $100   **c.** each $1,000 _____

2. The price of 1 pound of coffee in January is 1976, $1.60; 1978, $3.50; 1980, $3.25; 1982, $2.50; 1984, $2.60.
   a. each $.10   **b.** each $.20   **c.** each $.50 _____

3. Make a broken-line graph for exercise 1.   4. Make a broken-line graph for exercise 2.

Broken-Line Graphs

A person of what early language group spoke the language that became today's Irish, Highland Scottish, and Welsh languages?

Monthly Normal Rainfall for Tampa, Florida

To solve:
1. Work each exercise.
2. Find each answer in the clue box and cross out the letter above the answer. Some of the letters have already been crossed out.
3. Transfer the letters that are not crossed out, in order, to the answer below.

Example: **1.** How many inches of rainfall does the side of a small square indicate on the vertical scale of the line graph?

Solution: 1   Cross out the letter G above 1.

How many inches of rainfall are indicated by each of the following?

  2. 4 squares _____   **3.** 5.5 squares _____   **4.** 4.5 squares _____

  5. In which month is the amount of rainfall greatest? _____

  6. In which month is the amount of rainfall least? _____

In which month is the amount of rainfall closest to each of the following months?

  7. September _____   **8.** October _____   **9.** July _____

Find the normal amount of rainfall for each of the following months.

  10. March _____   **11.** November _____   **12.** September _____

  13. February _____   **14.** December _____   **15.** July _____

  16. January _____   **17.** June _____   **18.** August _____

A	B	C	D	E	F	Ø	H	I	J	K	L	M
JAN	2.5	9.5	8.5	FEB	2.5	1	4.5	3.5	4	7	1.5	3.5
N	O	P	Ø	R	S	T	Ø	V	W	X	Y	Z
MAY	6.5	5.5	0.5	AUG	2	NOV	9	JULY	8	5	JUNE	6

NAME _____ CLASS _____ DATE _____

Bar Graphs

Name the Zapotec Indian who rose from poverty to become President of Mexico from 1858 until his death in 1872.

To solve:

1. Work each exercise.
2. Find each answer below.
3. Write the letter of the exercise above the answer.

Example: **A.** In the title to the graph on the right, how many states are pictured?

Solution: 9   Write *A* above 9.

Find the percent of land forested in each state.

O. Connecticut _____

L. New Jersey _____

P. Arkansas _____

J. Wyoming _____

E. Maine _____

B. Ohio _____

R. Florida _____

N. Utah _____

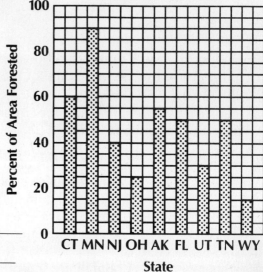

Percent of Land Area Forested in Nine States

U. Which state has the largest percent of land forested? _____

Z. Which state has the smallest percent of land forested? _____

I. Which state has the same percent of land forested as Florida? _____

T. Which state has more land forested, Ohio or Utah? _____

							A			
25	90	30	TN	UH	60		55	9	25	40	60

		A			
15	MN	9	50	90	WY

Data Analysis

Circle Graphs

In 1937, the first woman to fly alone across the Atlantic
Ocean was lost attempting a solo flight around the world.
Who was she and where was she last seen?

To solve:
1. Work each exercise.
2. Find each answer below.
3. Write the letter of the exercise above the answer.

Origin of Zoo Animals

North America 30%
Africa 25%
Asia 12.5%
Australia 7.5%
Europe 5%
South America 20%

Example: **M.** What percent of zoo animals come from Europe?

Solution: 5%   Write *M* above 5%.

What percent of zoo animals come from each region?

A. South America _____   **I.** Africa _____   **L.** Australia _____

What fraction of zoo animals come from each region?

E. South America _____   **W.** Africa _____   **E.** North America _____

R. Europe _____   **U.** Asia _____   **H.** Australia _____

Solve.

N. If there are 150 zoo animals, how many are from North America? _____

G. If there are 136 zoo animals, how many are from Africa? _____

A. If there are 360 zoo animals, how many are from Europe? _____

T. If there are 224 zoo animals, how many are from Asia? _____

___ $\frac{M}{}$ ___ ___ ___ ___   ___ ___ ___ ___ ___ ___ ___,
18 5% $\frac{1}{5}$ $7\frac{1}{2}$% 25% 18 $\frac{3}{10}$ 18 $\frac{1}{20}$ $\frac{3}{40}$ 20% $\frac{1}{20}$ 28

LAST SEEN IN   ___ ___ ___   ___ ___ ___ ___ ___ ___
                 45 $\frac{1}{5}$ $\frac{1}{4}$ 34 $\frac{1}{8}$ 25% 45 $\frac{3}{10}$ 20%

Data Analysis

Circle Graphs

Choosing the Most Appropriate Graph

Use the following guidelines to choose the most appropriate graph
to display specific data.

Line Graphs

- Data are continuous.
- Intermediate values have meaning.

   In the graph at the right, intermediate values between
   2 centimeters on Day 2 and 4 centimeters on Day 3 are
   significant.

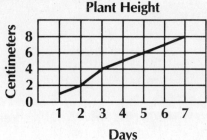

Plant Height

Bar Graphs

- Data are not continuous.
- Intermediate values have no meaning.

   In the graph at the right, a value of 2.5 hours between
   Monday and Tuesday is not significant.

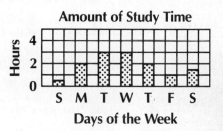

Amount of Study Time

Circle Graphs

- Parts are compared to the whole and to each other.
- The circle represents the whole.
- Each sector represents a proportional part or a percentage of
  the whole.

In the graph at the right, 25% of the students walk to school
and are represented by 25% of the circle.

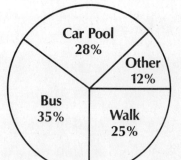

Transportation to School

Determine which kind of graph is most appropriate.

1. Show the number of students enrolled in each grade at a particular high school. _____

2. Compare the cost of a telephone call with the length of the call. _____

3. Show the number of winning games for different soccer teams during a season. _____

4. Show the depths reached by a deep sea diver during various dives. _____

5. Show the monthly sales of all the departments in a store. _____

6. Compare the increase in typing speed with the number of hours of practice. _____

7. Show the average hours of sunlight for each month during one year. _____

Circle Graphs

Divisions of a Circle Graph

Make a circle graph to show the following data. The number of
skiers at Sun Ski Area for one week was Monday to Thursday,
5,000; Friday, 3,750; Saturday, 6,250; and Sunday, 10,000.

Make a table to show the given data, the percent each quantity
is of the whole, and the number of degrees of a circle
representing each percent.

Day	Skiers	Percent	Degrees in the graph
Monday to Thursday	5,000	20%	72°
Friday	3,750	15%	54°
Saturday	6,250	25%	90°
Sunday	10,000	40%	144°
Total	25,000	100%	360°

Divide the number of skiers each
day by the total number of
skiers to obtain the percent.

A circle has 360°. To find the angle to represent
each day, multiply 360° by each percent.

Divide the circle into the angles listed in the table.
Label each section.

**Complete the table below. Round to the nearest degree. Then
construct a circle graph.**

THE BUDGET DOLLAR

	Items	Amount	Percent	Degrees
1.	Health Insurance	$.30	_____	_____
2.	Income Tax	$.45	_____	_____
3.	Corporate Tax	$.12	_____	_____
4.	Excise Tax	$.06	_____	_____
5.	Other	$.07	_____	_____
6.	Total	_____	_____	_____

Data Analysis

Range and Measures of Central Tendency

Name the Italian navigator who sailed into New York in 1524 and named newly discovered places after people and places in his homeland.

To solve:
1. Work each exercise.
2. Find the first digit to the left of the clue box. Find the second digit above the clue box. Find the letter at the intersection of the row and column.
3. Write that letter above the number of the exercise below.

	2	3	4	5	8
1	N	E	I	A	R
2	T	O	S	D	C
3	N	I	V	O	R
5	P	O	I	A	G
7	A	Z	D	V	N

Example: 1. Find the mean of 74 and 82.

Solution: 78   The letter at the intersection of 7 and 8 is *N*.
Write *N* above 1.

Find the mean for each list of scores.

2. 61, 50, 47, 54 _____

3. 75, 68, 77, 70, 80 _____

4. 87, 48, 96, 77, 50, 75, 71 _____

5. 64, 59, 69, 53, 62, 46, 53 _____

Find the median for each list of scores.

6. 35, 32, 41, 44, 28, 34, 30 _____

7. 75, 76, 67, 65, 70, 77, 73, 63, 79 _____

8. 41, 46, 64, 54, 25, 68, 37, 29, 61, 75, 57 _____

Find the range for each list of scores.

9. 80, 79, 85, 75, 84, 76, 88, 80 _____

10. 37, 39, 36, 40, 42, 37, 51, 39, 45, 54, 36, 44, 41, 50 _____

___ ___ ___ ___ ___ _N_ _N_ ___   ___ ___
 5   8   2   6   4   1   1   8   3   4

___ ___ ___ ___ ___ ___ ___ _N_ ___
 6   9 10 10   4   7   4   1   2

Range and Measures of Central Tendency

The Plot Thickens in the Middle

If you arrange data in order from least to greatest, the median divides the data into two groups of equal size. The median of the lower half is called the *lower quartile*. The median of the upper half is called the *upper quartile*. The median and the lower and upper quartiles divide the data into four groups of approximately equal size. You can use the median and the lower and upper quartiles to make a *box plot* that shows the central tendency of the data.

Example: Students who took a math quiz received the scores listed below. Make a box plot to show the central tendency of the scores.

3, 3, 6, 7, 7, 9, 9, 10, 10, 12, 12, 12, 13, 14, 14, 14, 15, 20

Lower Extreme | Lower Quartile | Median | Upper Quartile | Upper Extreme

Solution:
- Draw a number line labeling the numbers at evenly spaced intervals. Make dots below the line at each of the two extremes, at each of the two quartiles, and at the median.

- Draw a box with a length that is the distance between the two quartiles. Draw a line through the box at the median.

- Draw two line segments from the quartiles to the extremes.

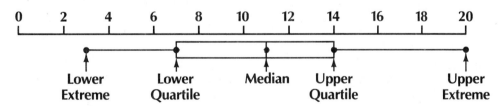

The students in gym class received the following tests scores.

Coordination: 4, 5, 6, 6, 7, 9, 10, 10, 10, 12, 13, 13, 14, 14, 15, 18, 18, 19
Endurance: 2, 2, 3, 3, 3, 5, 6, 6, 6, 8, 8, 8, 9, 10, 10, 10, 11, 15

Complete the chart. Then make a box plot that shows the central tendency for each set of test scores.

	Median	Lower Quartile	Upper Quartile	Lower Extreme	Upper Extreme
Coordination					
Endurance					

Rational Numbers

Absolute Value

The absolute value of any number is its distance from 0 on the number line without regard to the direction.

$|-3|$ means the absolute value of negative three.
$|-3| = 3$ and $|+3| = 3$

Opposites have the same absolute value and different signs.

$+5$ is the absolute opposite of -5.
-13 is the opposite of $+13$.

What number is the opposite?

1. 10 _____

2. $-\frac{1}{2}$ _____

3. -28 _____

4. 45 _____

5. 6.75 _____

6. -7.005 _____

7. -107 _____

8. $+\frac{3}{21}$ _____

9. $+1,250$ _____

10. $-50\frac{1}{4}$ _____

11. $+\frac{7}{2}$ _____

12. -20.45 _____

Find the absolute value.

13. $|+10|$ _____

14. $|-6|$ _____

15. $|+\frac{1}{2}|$ _____

16. $|-8.3|$ _____

17. $|+54|$ _____

18. $|-\frac{7}{9}|$ _____

19. $|-0.081|$ _____

20. $|+4\frac{4}{5}|$ _____

21. $|+4.06|$ _____

22. $|-1.91|$ _____

23. $|-87.4|$ _____

24. $|+3,268|$ _____

List all of the numbers described by the following.

23. $2, 3, 4, \ldots, 10$ _____

26. $-8, -7, -6, \ldots, -1$ _____

27. $-4, -3, -2, \ldots, 4$ _____

NAME _____ CLASS _____ DATE _____

Rational Numbers

According to Sigmund Freud, who first proposed its existence, this is the part of our personality that is conscious, that most immediately controls behavior, and that is not in touch with external reality. What is it called?

To solve:

1. Work each exercise.
2. Find each answer below and cross out the letter above the answer. Some letters have already been crossed out.
3. Transfer letters that are not crossed out, in order, to the answer below.

Example: 1. Write negative three-fourths using symbols.

Solution: $-\frac{3}{4}$ Cross out the letter J above $-\frac{3}{4}$.

Write using symbols.

2. negative three _____

3. positive five-eighths _____

4. positive forty-two hundredths _____

5. negative one-third _____

6. negative seven-tenths _____

7. positive fourteen _____

What number is the opposite of each of the following?

8. -5.45 _____

9. $\frac{2}{9}$ _____

10. $+3\frac{3}{7}$ _____

11. -0.005 _____

12. -6.006 _____

13. $+2\frac{1}{10}$ _____

Find the absolute value of each of the following.

14. $\left|+\frac{8}{5}\right|$ _____

15. $|-15|$

16. $|-0.025|$

17. $\left|-6\frac{2}{3}\right|$ _____

18. $|-141.3|$

19. $\left|+\frac{13}{484}\right|$ _____

A	B	C	D	E	F	G	H	I	J̶	K	L	M
$+5.45$	$-2\frac{1}{10}$	$+0.025$	$+\frac{5}{8}$	$+0.7$	$-\frac{2}{9}$	$-6\frac{2}{3}$	$-\frac{1}{3}$	$+0.005$	$-\frac{3}{4}$	$+15$	$+6.006$	-0.7
N	O	P	Q	R	S	T	U̶	V̶	W	X	Y	Z
$-3\frac{3}{7}$	$+\frac{3}{4}$	-3	$+141.3$	$+14$	$+\frac{8}{5}$	$+0.42$	-5.45	$-\frac{5}{8}$	$+6\frac{2}{3}$	$+\frac{1}{3}$	$+\frac{13}{484}$	$+2\frac{1}{10}$

Rational Numbers and Integers

Graphing on a Number Line

Draw the graph of −3, −5, and 6 on the number line.

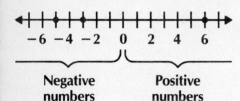

-6 -4 -2 0 2 4 6

Negative numbers   **Positive numbers**

Remember, negative numbers are to the left of zero and positive numbers are to the right of zero.

First, move 3 units to the left of zero to locate −3.

Next, move 5 units to the left of zero to locate −5.

Now, move six units to the right of zero to locate 6.

What letter labels the point corresponding to each number?

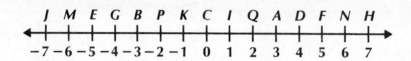

J M E G B P K C I Q A D F N H
-7 -6 -5 -4 -3 -2 -1 0 1 2 3 4 5 6 7

1. −4 _____	**2.** 0 _____	**3.** −5 _____	**4.** 7 _____
5. −7 _____	**6.** 3 _____	**7.** −1 _____	**8.** −3 _____

Draw the graph of each set of numbers on a number line.

9. 5, −3

-7 -6 -5 -4 -3 -2 -1 0 1 2 3 4 5 6 7

10. −6, −2, 3

-7 -6 -5 -4 -3 -2 -1 0 1 2 3 4 5 6 7

11. −4, 0, 6, −1, 2

-7 -6 -5 -4 -3 -2 -1 0 1 2 3 4 5 6 7

Write the coordinates of each graph.

12.

-7 -6 -5 -4 -3 -2 -1 0 1 2 3 4 5 6 7   _____

13.

-7 -6 -5 -4 -3 -2 -1 0 1 2 3 4 5 6 7   _____

14.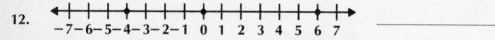

-7 -6 -5 -4 -3 -2 -1 0 1 2 3 4 5 6 7   _____

NAME _____ CLASS _____ DATE _____

Comparing Integers

Insert the correct symbol (<, >, or =) to make a true sentence.

−9 ____ −4

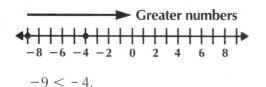 Greater numbers

−9 < − 4.

Draw the graph of both numbers on a number line. The greater numbers are to the right. −4 is to the right of −9.
So −4 is greater than −9, and −9 is less than −4.

Draw the graph of the following numbers on a number line. Then write <, >, or = to make a true sentence.

1. −1 ____ −6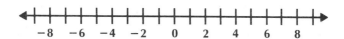

2. −5 ____ −9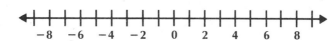

3. −9 ____ 0

4. −6 ____ −4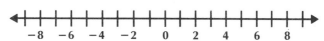

Circle the number that is greater.

5. −3 or 12   6. 32 or −40   7. 0 or 4   8. 0 or −7

9. −2 or −4   10. 8 or −6   11. 0 or −10   12. −3 or 3

Circle the number that is less.

13. −6 or −8   14. 9 or −11   15. 0 or −3   16. 4 or 8

17. 2 or 0   18. −5 or −3   19. −1 or −11   20. −9 or −2

Write true or false.

21. −2 > −6 _____   22. 8 > −2 _____   23. −5 > −1 _____

24. 0 < −4 _____   25. +7 > +9 _____   26. $|-5| < 5$ _____

27. $|-2| > 1$ _____   28. −5 < −6 _____   29. $|-8| = 8$ _____

Comparing Integers

Comparing and Ordering Rational Numbers

You can use a number line to compare and order positive and negative fractions and mixed numbers.

Example: Compare $-\frac{1}{3}$ and $-\frac{2}{5}$.

Solution: Write the fractions with a common denominator.

$$-\frac{1}{3} = -\frac{5}{15} \qquad -\frac{2}{5} = -\frac{6}{15}$$

Compare the fractions on a number line.

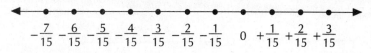

$$-\frac{5}{15} > -\frac{6}{15}$$
So, $-\frac{1}{3} > -\frac{2}{5}$.

Compare these rational numbers. Write < or >.

1. $\frac{2}{3}$ ____ $\frac{5}{7}$

2. $-1\frac{3}{4}$ ____ $-1\frac{7}{9}$

3. $2\frac{4}{7}$ ____ $2\frac{5}{9}$

4. $-\frac{1}{3}$ ____ $-\frac{2}{7}$

5. $-5\frac{5}{9}$ ____ $-5\frac{3}{4}$

6. $3\frac{4}{5}$ ____ $3\frac{3}{4}$

List these rational numbers in order from least to greatest.

7. $\frac{2}{3}, \frac{3}{4}, \frac{7}{12}, \frac{1}{4}, \frac{3}{8}, \frac{1}{3}, \frac{1}{12}, \frac{1}{8}, \frac{5}{6}, \frac{5}{12}$

_____

8. $-1\frac{1}{2}, -1\frac{3}{4}, -1\frac{1}{3}, -1\frac{5}{12}, -1\frac{5}{6}, -1\frac{2}{3}$

_____

List these elevations from highest to lowest.

9. $13\frac{1}{2}$ feet above sea level, $12\frac{1}{3}$ feet below sea level, $15\frac{1}{4}$ feet below sea level, $12\frac{3}{4}$ feet below sea level, $13\frac{1}{3}$ feet above sea level, $12\frac{1}{2}$ feet above sea level, $15\frac{1}{3}$ feet below sea level, $12\frac{5}{6}$ feet above sea level

_____

_____

NAME _____ CLASS _____ DATE _____

Adding Integers and Rational Numbers

Adding Numbers with Opposite Signs

Find the sum of −5 and +6.

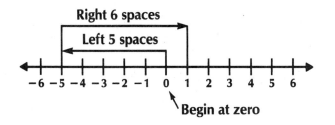

Right 6 spaces
Left 5 spaces

Begin at zero

Use a number line to help.
Begin at zero. Move left for negative and right for positive.
Move left 5 spaces for −5.
Now, move right 6 spaces for +6.
Read the answer.

$(-5) + (+6) = +1$

Use a number line to find each sum.

1. $(-7) + (+3)$ _____
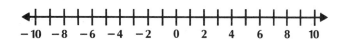

2. $(-5) + (-4)$ _____
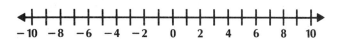

3. $(-4) + (+8)$ _____
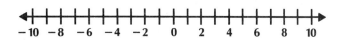

4. $(+2) + (-6)$ _____
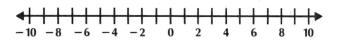

5. $(-5) + (+5)$ _____
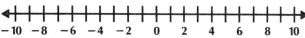

Add. Use the number line if you need it.

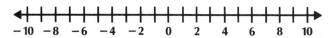

6. $(-8) + (-6)$ _____ **7.** $(+7) + (+8)$ _____ **8.** $(-9) + (+2)$ _____

9. $(+11) + (-7)$ _____ **10.** $(-13) + (+5)$ _____ **11.** $(+6) + (-18)$ _____

12. $(+21) + (-19)$ _____ **13.** $(-8) + (-7)$ _____ **14.** $(+11) + (+16)$ _____

15. $(-18) + (-11)$ _____ **16.** $(-9) + (+6)$ _____ **17.** $(-8) + (+8)$ _____

Rational Numbers and Integers

Additive Inverse of a Number

Additive Inverse of Negative Numbers

Find the additive inverse of −6.

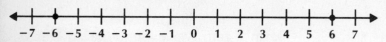

Draw a number line.
Locate −6.
The opposite of −6 is +6.
Locate +6.
The additive inverse is the same as the opposite.

The additive inverse of −6 is +6.

Locate each number on the number line, then find the additive inverse.

1. −4 _____

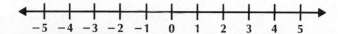

2. −5 _____

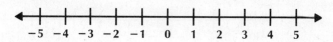

3. −1.5 _____

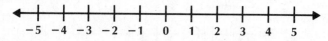

4. −3 _____

Write the additive inverse.

5. −100 _____   **6.** +23.5 _____   **7.** $+\frac{2}{3}$ _____

8. $-\frac{1}{2}$ _____   **9.** −0.23 _____   **10.** −5.346 _____

Match each expression with its symbolic value.

11. The additive inverse of negative ten. _____

12. The additive inverse of ten. _____

13. The additive inverse of thirty-two. _____

14. The additive inverse of negative eighteen. _____

15. The additive inverse of negative forty-three. _____

a. −18
b. −32
c. +43
d. −10
e. −43
f. −(−18)
g. −(−10)
h. +32

NAME _____ CLASS _____ DATE _____

Subtracting Integers and Rational Numbers

Subtracting Numbers with Opposite Signs

Subtract: $(+6) - (-3)$

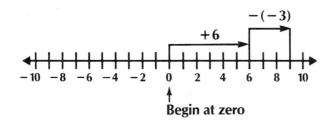

Begin at zero

Use a number line to help.
Begin at zero. Move left for negative and right for positive.
Move right 6 spaces for +6.
When you subtract, move in the opposite direction of the sign of the number.
To subtract −3, move right 3 spaces.
Read the answer.

$(+6) - (-3) = +9$

Subtract. Use a number line to help.

1. $(-5) - (-8)$ _____
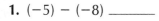

2. $(+4) - (-3)$ _____

3. $(-5) - (+5)$ _____

4. $(+6) - (+1)$ _____

5. $(-3) - (+7)$ _____

Subtract. Use the number line if you need it.

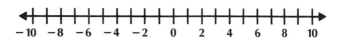
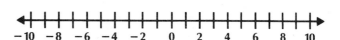
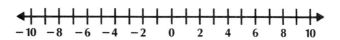
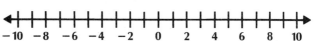
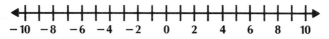

6. $(-8) - (-2)$ _____   **7.** $(+11) - (+5)$ _____   **8.** $(+6) - (+18)$ _____

9. $(-11) - (-21)$ _____   **10.** $(-5) - (+8)$ _____   **11.** $(-3.5) - (+2)$ _____

12. $(+2.1) - (+5.3)$ _____   **13.** $(0) - (-14)$ _____   **14.** $(-2) - (+1\frac{1}{2})$ _____

Subtracting Integers and Rational Numbers

Midway through law school, this Bostonian shipped to California as a common sailor. Later, he wrote of his adventures in *Two Years Before the Mast*, one of the greatest, most realistic sea stories ever written. Name the author.

To solve:

1. Work each exercise.
2. Find the digits of each answer on the corresponding number line. (Note that there are different number lines for positive and negative answers.) Cross out the letter that matches each digit. Some letters may be crossed out more than once.
3. Transfer letters that are not crossed out, in order, to the answer below.

Example: 1. Subtract: $(+4) - (+30)$

Solution: -26 On answer line II, cross out the letters above 2 and 6.

Subtract. Use number lines I and II.

2. $(+78) - (+2)$ _____   3. $(+40) - (+20)$ _____

4. $(-45) - (-7)$ _____   5. $(-27) - (+18)$ _____

6. $(-13) - (-51)$ _____   7. $(+57.1) - (-37)$ _____

8. $(-11) - (+8)$ _____   9. $(+47) - (+84)$ _____

Subtract. Use number lines III and IV.

10. $(-26.4) - (+9)$ _____   11. $(+2.2) - (-4.6)$ _____

12. $(+14.1) - (-33)$ _____   13. $(-37.8) - (-8)$ _____

14. $(+5) - (+22)$ _____   15. $(-7) - (-27)$ _____

16. $(+18) - (-41)$ _____   17. $(-10) - (+30)$ _____

RICHARD   HENRY   __ __ __ __

line line line line
I   II   III IV

Positive

Negative

Positive

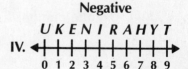

Negative

U K E N I R A H Y T

IV. ⬅+++++++++➡
    0 1 2 3 4 5 6 7 8 9

NAME _____ CLASS _____ DATE _____

Multiplying Integers and Rational Numbers

Correct Answer Sign

Multiply: $(-8)(-6)$

$(-8)(-6) = +48$ When the signs are alike, the product is positive.

Multiply: $(+8)(+6)$

$(+8)(+6) = +48$ When the signs are alike, the product is positive.

Multiply: $(-8)(+6)$

$(-8)(+6) = -48$ When the signs are different, the product is negative.

Write + or −.

1. $(+2)(+5) = $ ___ 10   2. $(-2)(-5) = $ ___ 10   3. $(+2)(-5) = $ ___ 10

4. $(-4)(-6) = $ ___ 24   5. $(+4)(+6) = $ ___ 24   6. $(-4)(+6) = $ ___ 24

7. $(+9)(+3) = $ ___ 27   8. $(-9)(-3) = $ ___ 27   9. $(+9)(-3) = $ ___ 27

Multiply.

10. $(-6)(+5)$ ___   11. $(-8)(-7)$ ___   12. $(+9)(+6)$ ___

13. $(-10)(-5)$ ___   14. $(+8)(-9)$ ___   15. $(-12)(+11)$ ___

16. $(-10)(-15)$ ___   17. $(+6)(-7)$ ___   18. $(-18)(-3)$ ___

19. $(+5)(-9)$ ___   20. $(-6)(+12)$ ___   21. $(-7)(-7)$ ___

22. $(-2)(+8)(+3)$ ___   23. $(-3)(-2)(-10)$ ___

24. $(+1)(-5)(-3)$ ___   25. $(-1)(+2)(-5)$ ___

Find the value.

26. $|-5| \times |+10|$ ___   27. $|-2| \times |+1|$ ___

28. $|+4(-6)| \times (0)$ ___   29. $(-1) \times |-3|$ ___

Dividing Integers and Rational Numbers

Correct Answer Sign

Divide: $(-12) \div (-3)$

$(-12) \div (-3) = +4$ When the signs are alike,
$\dfrac{-12}{-3} = +4$ the quotient is positive.

Divide: $(+12) \div (+3)$

$(+12) \div (+3) = +4$ When the signs are alike,
$\dfrac{+12}{+3} = +4$ the quotient is positive.

Divide: $(-12) \div (+3)$

$(-12) \div (+3) = -4$ When the signs are different,
$\dfrac{-12}{+3} = -4$ the quotient is negative.

Write + or −.

1. $(-16) \div (+8) = \underline{\quad} 2$
2. $(+48) \div (+6) = \underline{\quad} 8$
3. $(+25) \div (-5) = \underline{\quad} 5$
4. $\dfrac{-32}{-4} = \underline{\quad} 8$
5. $\dfrac{-16}{-4} = \underline{\quad} 4$
6. $\dfrac{+72}{-9} = \underline{\quad} 8$

Divide.

7. $\dfrac{-22}{-11}$ _____
8. $\dfrac{+27}{-9}$ _____
9. $\dfrac{-80}{-5}$ _____
10. $(+210) \div (+10)$ _____
11. $(-1.44) \div (+1.2)$ _____
12. $(-40) \div (-1)$ _____
13. $\dfrac{0}{-18}$ ____
14. $\dfrac{+80}{-1}$ _____
15. $\dfrac{-54}{+6}$ _____
16. $(-49) \div (-7)$ _____
17. $(+132) \div (+11)$ _____
18. $(+108) \div (-12)$ _____
19. $\dfrac{-104}{+8}$ _____
20. $\dfrac{+2.4}{-0.6}$ _____
21. $\dfrac{-5.4}{+0.9}$ _____
22. $(-4.2) \div (+0.06)$ _____
23. $(-85) \div (-5)$ _____
24. $(+8.8) \div (-1.1)$ _____
25. $\dfrac{+60}{-5}$ _____
26. $\dfrac{+18}{-5}$ _____
27. $\dfrac{-63}{-9}$ _____
28. $(+96) \div (-3)$ _____
29. $(-54) \div (-2)$ _____
30. $(+48) \div (+12)$ _____

NAME _____ CLASS _____ DATE _____

Estimation/Mental Math

What number is the opposite?

1. $+0.09$ _____   **2.** $+\frac{3}{5}$ _____

3. $+213.27$ _____   **4.** $-7\frac{2}{3}$ _____

Write true or false.

(≯ means "not greater than"; ≮ means "not less than.")

5. $-7 \not> -2$ _____   **6.** $-7 \not< 0$ _____   **7.** $+4 \not> -4$ _____
8. $10 \not< 10$ _____   **9.** $-24 \not< -7$ _____   **10.** $-15 \not> -17$ _____

Mentally find the value.

11. $-(-3.5)$ _____   **12.** $-(+37.3)$ _____

13. $-\left(\frac{9}{7}\right)$ _____   **14.** $(+12) + (-3)$ _____

15. $\left(+\frac{5}{8}\right) + \left(+\frac{1}{4}\right)$ _____   **16.** $-20 + 0$ _____

17. $(+42) - (-38)$ _____   **18.** $(-56) - (-16)$ _____

19. $(-4)(+8)$ _____   **20.** $-6(-3 - 1)$ _____

21. $(-40)(-20)$ _____   **22.** $(-20)(400)$ _____

23. $(-2)^3$ _____   **24.** $5 \times 2^2 \times (-5)^2$ _____

25. $(-182) \div (14)$ _____   **26.** $(-77) \div 7$ _____

27. $(261) \div (-9)$ _____   **28.** $(-9)^2 \div (-9) \div (-3)$ _____

29. $(-81) \div (-9) \div (-3)$ _____   **30.** $8\,[2 + (-22)]$ _____

31. $\dfrac{(-2)^3 - (4)^2}{(-5)^2}$ _____   **32.** $\dfrac{5(4 - 6) - 7(5 - 10)}{-1 - (-6)}$ _____

33. The sum of an integer and -24 is -56. Find the integer. _____

34. The product of what number and $+12$ is -48? _____

35. A number is divided by $+5$, then divided by $+5$. The result is -1. What is the

number? _____

Calculator

The change sign ($\boxed{+/-}$) key on a calculator allows you to perform operations with negative and positive numbers. When $\boxed{+/-}$ is pressed, any number is converted to its opposite. That is, a positive number becomes negative and a negative number becomes positive, without any change in the digits or placement of the decimal point.

Enter each of the following on a calculator and simplify.

−4   4 $\boxed{+/-}$ −4

−(−5)   5 $\boxed{+/-}$ $\boxed{+/-}$ 5

(−9) + 6   9 $\boxed{+/-}$ $\boxed{+}$ 6 $\boxed{=}$ −3

(−5) × (−3)   5 $\boxed{+/-}$ $\boxed{\times}$ 3 $\boxed{+/-}$ = 15

When a negative number is stored in the calculator's memory, the negative sign appears as a line under the "M" in the display.

Find each of the following.

(4 − 9) + (2 − 3)   4 $\boxed{-}$ 9 $\boxed{M+}$ 2 $\boxed{-}$ 3 $\boxed{M+}$ $\boxed{M\genfrac{}{}{0pt}{}{R}{C}}$ $^M6$

(4 − 9) + (2 − 3) = −6

81 − 5^{4M} 81 $\boxed{M+}$ 5 $\boxed{\times}\boxed{=}\boxed{=}\boxed{=}$ $\boxed{+/-}$ $\boxed{M+}$ = −544

Use a calculator to find each of the following.

1. −1 + (−4) + 6 + (−3) + 5 _____

2. (−8) − (5) _____

3. (−92)(−3.4) _____

4. (−7)(2)(−15) _____

5. (+0.56) ÷ (−0.7) _____

6. (−343) ÷ (−7) _____

7. 4,914 ÷ (−18) _____

8. (−1.4) × (5.6) × (−0.3) _____

9. (279 − 560) + (−4)^2 _____

10. −$\sqrt{7,056}$ + 6^3 − (29 ÷ 5) _____

11. −3.58 + 1.39 _____

12. +3.6 + (−2.9) + (−4.39) _____

13. −8(4 − 5) − (1 − 5) _____

14. (−2)^4 × (−3)^2 _____

15. −(4^2) × (−6)(−2) _____

16. $(-7\frac{1}{5}) \div (+\frac{1}{10})$ _____

17. [36 ÷ (−4)] ÷ (−4) ÷ (−4) + $\sqrt{961}$ _____

18. If Mary's watch loses 75 seconds each day, how much time does it lose in a week? (Express your answer in minutes.) _____

NAME _____ CLASS _____ DATE _____

Algebraic Expressions

In *As You Like It*, what did William Shakespeare write when he compared life to a play?

To solve:

1. Work each exercise.
2. In the clue box find the word that matches each answer.
3. Write that word above the number of the exercise below.

$4 + 2$—and	$5 - k$—players
$10 - 6$—the	$5 + k$—a
xy—merely	$5(g + k)$—all
$3m$—women	$\frac{1}{5}(g + k)$—men
m^2—world's	$\frac{5}{g + k}$—and
$\frac{x}{y}$—the	$b^2 + h$—stage
$\sqrt{m}$—all	

Example: **1.** Write as an algebraic expression: two added to four.

Solution: $4 + 2$ The word *and* matches $4 + 2$. Write *and* above 1.

Write each of the following as an algebraic expression.

2. from ten subtract six _____

3. the square root of m _____

4. the product of 3 and m _____

5. x times y _____

6. five plus k _____

7. m squared _____

8. the difference between 5 and k _____

9. the sum of b squared and h _____

10. one-fifth the sum of g and k _____

11. the quotient of five divided by the sum of g and k _____

12. five times the sum of g and k _____

13. the quotient of x and y _____

"_____ _____ _____ _____ _____ ,
　　　3　　　　　　13　　　　　7　　　　　　6　　　　　9

_____ _____ _____ _____ _____
　　AND　　　　　12　　　　　2　　　　　10　　　　　11
　　　1

_____ _____ _____ _____ . . ."
　　　4　　　　　5　　　　　8

Algebra

Evaluating Expressions

Order of Operations

Find the value of $3(a - 6) + x^2$ when $a = 15$ and $x = 7$.

$3(a - 6) + x^2$	
$3(15 - 6) + 7^2$	Substitute the given variables.

Remember the correct order of operations.

$3(15 - 6) + 49$	**1.** Compute squares or cubes of numbers.
$3(9) + 49$	**2.** Do any operations within parentheses.
$27 + 49$	**3.** Multiply and divide.
76	**4.** Add and subtract.

Choose the correct value of each algebraic expression.

1. $3x - z$ when $x = 5$ and $z = 2$
  a. $3(2) - 5$ **b.** $3(5) - 2$ **c.** $5 - 2$ _____

2. $5(a + 2c)$ when $a = 7$ and $c = 4$
  a. $5(7 + 2 \cdot 4)$ **b.** $5(4 + 2 \cdot 4)$ **c.** $5 + 2(7)$ _____

3. $3z(8 - x)$ when $z = 6$ and $x = 2$
  a. $3(6)(8 - 2)$ **b.** $3(8 - 6)$ **c.** $3(6)(8 - 6)$ _____

4. $(a + b)^2$ when $a = 5$ and $b = 3$
  a. 34 **b.** 64 **c.** 225 _____

Find the value of each algebraic expression when $a = 5$ and $b = 7$.

5. $4a - 2b$ _____   **6.** $4(2b - a)$ _____   **7.** $a^2 + b^2$ _____

8. $(b - a)^2$ _____   **9.** $7ab$ _____   **10.** $3a^2b$ _____

11. $\dfrac{a + b}{3a - b}$ _____   **12.** $2a^2 - ab$ _____   **13.** $5b \div a$ _____

Find the value of each algebraic expression when $x = 8$ and $y = 12$.

14. $x^2 + 2$ _____   **15.** $x + y - 10$ _____   **16.** xy _____

17. $4(y - 6)$ _____   **18.** $y^2 - x^2$ _____   **19.** $4y \div x$ _____

Evaluating Formulas

Alexandre Dumas wrote *The Three Musketeers.* Athos was one of the musketeers. Name the other two.

To solve:
1. Work each exericse.
2. Find the first two digits of each answer to the left of the answer box. Find the third digit above the answer box.
3. Write the letter of the exercise in the box at the intersection of the row and column.

Example: **P.** Using the formula $d = 2r$, find the value of d when $r = 180$.

Solution: $d = 360$ Write P at the intersection of 36 and 0.

Find the value.

R. A when $b = 37$ and $h = 13$. Formula: $A = bh$ _____

R. A when $m = 479$ and $n = 245$. Formula: $A = \frac{m + n}{2}$ _____

I. C when $\pi = \frac{22}{7}$ and $r = 77$. Formula: $C = 2\pi r$ _____

S. S when $a = 145$, $b = 79$, and $c = 142$. Formula: $S = a + b + c$ _____

H. V when $l = 13$, $w = 7$, and $h = 4$. Formula: $V = lwh$ _____

S. p when $s = 97$. Formula: $p = 5s$ _____

A. p when $l = 190$ and $w = 51$. Formula: $p = 2l + 2w$ _____

T. A when $h = 22$, $b_1 = 21$, and $b_2 = 12$. Formula: $A = \frac{1}{2} h(b_1 + b_2)$ _____

A. i when $p = 8$, $r = 5$, and $t = 12$. Formula: $i = prt$ _____

O. F when $C = 185$. Formula: $f = 1.8C + 32$ _____

O. d when $g = 2$ and $t = 19$. Formula: $d = \frac{1}{2}gt^2$ _____

M. V when $N = 441$ Formula: $V = 23\sqrt{N}$ _____

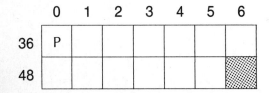

	0	1	2	3	4	5	6
36	P						
48							

Algebraic Sentences

What developed a crack in 1835 while tolling the death of U.S. Chief Justice John Marshall?

To solve:

1. Work each exercise.
2. In the clue box find the letter that matches each answer.
3. Write that letter above the number of the exercise each time it appears below.

$5n \ngtr 15$—L	$x + 4 = 9$—H
$5 + n \neq 5$—I	$x + 9 < 4$—V
$2n - 5 = 8$—E	$2x - 3 \geq 6$—Y
$\frac{5n}{8} < 1$—B	$\frac{x}{4} \nless 9$—R
$5 - n \geq 5$—L	$2x + 3 \leq 6$—B
$5 < n < 8$—P	$\frac{x}{4} = 9$—T
$\frac{8}{5n} \nless 1$—C	$4 < x < 9$—L
$2n + 8 > 5$—E	

Example: 1. Write as an algebraic sentence using symbols: Some number x plus four is equal to nine.

Solution: $x + 4 = 9$ The letter H matches this answer. Write H above 1.

Write each of the following as an algebraic sentence using symbols.

2. Two times some number n decreased by five is equal to eight. _____

3. Five plus each number n is not equal to five. _____

4. Two times each number x plus three is less than or equal to six. _____

5. Five less each number n is greater than or equal to five. _____

6. Five times some number n is not greater than fifteen. _____

7. Each number x divided by four is not less than nine. _____

8. Two times each number n increased by eight is greater than five. _____

9. Each number x divided by four is equal to nine. _____

10. Two times some number x minus three is greater than or equal to six. _____

11. Each number x is greater than four and less than nine. _____

12. Five times some number n when divided by eight is less than one. _____

```
___  H   ___     ___  ___  ___  ___  ___  ___  ___     ___  ___  ___  ___
 9   1   2        5    3   12   8    7    9   10        4    8   11   6
```

Properties of Equality

Both Sides of an Equation

Solve the equation for x. $3x = 15$

$3x = 15$

$\dfrac{3x}{3} = \dfrac{15}{3}$ Divide by 3 so x stands alone.

$x = 5$ Remember to divide both sides of the equation by 3.

Choose the correct solution for each equation.

1. $x + 2 = 8$
   a. 2   **b.** 6   **c.** 8   _____

2. $y - 3 = 2$
   a. 5   **b.** 3   **c.** 2   _____

3. $4 + z = 7$
   a. 11   **b.** 8   **c.** 3   _____

Choose the first step to solve each equation.

4. $8n = 16$
   a. $\dfrac{8n}{8} = 16$ **b.** $\dfrac{8n}{8} = \dfrac{16}{8}$ **c.** $8n = \dfrac{16}{8}$ _____

5. $2n + 1 = 5$
   a. $\dfrac{2n}{2} + 1 = \dfrac{5}{2}$ **b.** $\dfrac{2n}{2} + 1 - 1 = \dfrac{5}{2}$ **c.** $2n + 1 - 1 = 5 - 1$ _____

6. $\dfrac{n}{3} + 5 = 9$
   a. $\dfrac{n}{3} - 5 = 9 - 5$ **b.** $\dfrac{n}{3} + 5 \times 3 = 9 \times 3$ **c.** $\dfrac{n}{3} + 5 - 5 = 9 - 5$ _____

7. $\dfrac{n}{5} = 8$
   a. $\dfrac{n}{5} \times 5 = 8 \times 5$ **b.** $\dfrac{n}{5} \times 5 = 8$ **c.** $\dfrac{n}{5} = 8 \times 5$ _____

What operation with what number do you use on both sides of the given equation to get an equivalent equation in simplest form? Write the equivalent equation.

8. $7a = 56$ _____

9. $12 + c = 20$ _____

_____   _____

Algebra

Solving Equations by Addition

How was the state of Massachusetts to be governed, according to the words of John Adams in 1779?

To solve:
1. Work each exercise.
2. Find the first digit of each answer to the left of the clue box. Find the second digit above the clue box. Find the letter at the intersection of the row and column.
3. Write that letter above the number of the exercise each time it appears below.

	0	2	4	6	8
1	R	V	N	A	N
2	G	N	E	O	A
3	O	T	F	L	M
4	T	S	E	O	W
5	D	M	A	F	E

Example: 1. Solve: $x - 6 = 8$

Solution: $x = 14$ The letter at the intersection of 1 and 4 is N. Write N above 1.

Solve.

2. $a - 5 = 25; a =$ _____

3. $b - 17 = 39; b =$ _____

4. $c - 11 = 35; c =$ _____

5. $d - 7 = 21; d =$ _____

6. $50 = f - 8; f =$ _____

7. $h - 16 = 16; h =$ _____

8. $26 = j - 24; j =$ _____

9. $42 = k - 12; k =$ _____

10. $m - 10 = 4; m =$ _____

11. $n - 30 = -6; n =$ _____

12. $t - 20 = -2; =$ _____

13. $w - 35.7 = 16.3; w =$ _____

14. $x - 10 = 0; x =$ _____

15. $z - 5\frac{1}{3} = 6\frac{2}{3}; z =$ _____

16. $a - 7 = 13; a =$ _____

17. $\frac{1}{2} = b - 41\frac{1}{2}; b =$ _____

18. $15.39 = c - 20.61; c =$ _____

19. $d - 70 = -22; d =$ _____

``
"__ __ __ __ __ __ __ __ __ __ __   __ __   __ __ __ __,
  5   16 2 15 11 14 12 13 6 10 7   4   3   18 5 19 17

__ _N_ __   __ __ __   __ __   __ __ __"
 9   1   8   10 2 7   4 3   13 6 12
``

Algebra

Solving Equations by Addition

Variable on the Right Side of an Equation

Solve: $-2.5 = n - 1.8$

$$-2.5 = n - 1.8$$

Determine what operation is indicated in the equation.
It is subtraction.
Undo subtraction with addition.

$$-2.5 + 1.8 = n - 1.8 + 1.8$$
$$-2.5 + 1.8 = n$$
$$-0.7 = n$$

Since 1.8 is subtracted from n, add 1.8 to both sides of the equation.
Solve for n.

Check your answer.

$$-2.5 = n - 1.8$$
$$-2.5 = -0.7 - 1.8$$
$$-2.5 = -2.5$$

Substitute -0.7 for n in the equation.

Choose the first step to solve each equation.

1. $n - 14 = 26$
   a. Add 14 to both sides.
   c. Add -14 to both sides.
   b. Subtract 14 from both sides.
   d. Subtract 26 from both sides. _____

2. $13.6 = n - 15.3$
   a. Add -15.3 to both sides.
   c. Add 15.3 to both sides.
   b. Subtract 15.3 from both sides.
   d. Subtract 13.6 from both sides. _____

Tell what to do to solve each equation. Do not solve.

3. $\$12.70 = n - \$3.68$ _____

4. $21 = n - 30$ _____

Solve and check.

5. $-14 = n - 16$ _____
6. $34.8 = a - 17.1$ _____
7. $-25 = c - 20$ _____
8. $-42 = a - 42$ _____
9. $0 = a - 15$ _____
10. $-7 = y - 2.4$ _____
11. $\frac{3}{5} = d - 7$ _____
12. $-11 = x - 37$ _____

Solving Equations by Subtraction

The author of *Moby-Dick,* advised any writer wishing to create great literature that "to produce a mighty book, you must choose a mighty theme." Name this author.

To solve:
1. Work each exercise.
2. Find each answer below.
3. Write the letter of the exercise above the answer.

Example: Solve: **E.** $x + 3 = 10$

Solution: $x = 7$ Write *E* above 7.

Solve.

L. $d + 9 = 20; d =$ _____

A. $k + 6 = 11; k =$ _____

H. $a + 18 = 51; a =$ _____

E. $r + 65 = 65; r =$ _____

M. $88 + h = 129; h =$ _____

E. $-15 = b + 42; b =$ _____

L. $3.8 + k = 12.6; k =$ _____

L. $h + 5 = 14; h =$ _____

R. $m + 31 = 50; m =$ _____

V. $a + 25 = 11; a =$ _____

M. $5\frac{3}{4} = n + 3\frac{7}{8}; n =$ _____

I. $13.4 + y = 21.1; y =$ _____

N. $x + 1\frac{5}{8} = 4\frac{3}{4}; x =$ _____

__	__	__	__	__	__
33	0	19	41	5	$3\frac{1}{8}$

__	__	__	__	__	__	__	E
$1\frac{7}{8}$	-57	9	-14	7.7	11	8.8	7

Algebra

Solving Equations by Subtraction

Variable on the Right Side of an Equation

Solve: $16 = a + 4$

$16 = a + 4$ — Decide what operation is indicated in the equation.
It is addition.
Undo addition with subtraction.

$16 - 4 = a + 4 - 4$ — Since 4 is added to a, subtract 4 from both sides of the equation.
$16 - 4 = a$ — Solve for a.
$12 = a$

Check your answer.

$16 = a + 4$
$16 = 12 + 4$ — Substitute 12 for a in the equation.
$16 = 16$

Choose the first step to solve each equation.

1. $15 = n + 8$
 a. Add 8 to both sides. **b.** Add 15 to both sides.
 c. Subtract 8 from both sides. **d.** Subtract 15 from both sides. _____

2. $0.9 + w = 21$
 a. Add 0.4 to both sides **b.** Subtract 0.9 from both sides.
 c. Subtract 21 from both sides. **d.** Add -21 to both sides. _____

Tell what to do to solve each equation, but do not solve.

3. $8.6 = 12.3 + n$ _____

_____

4. $7\frac{3}{5} = 2\frac{1}{2} + b$ _____

Solve and check.

5. $21 = a + 5$ _____   **6.** $4.3 = 2.9 + w$ _____

7. $11 = r + 4$ _____   **8.** $8 = x + 8$ _____

9. $16 = a + 7$ _____   **10.** $11\frac{2}{5} = 3\frac{1}{2} + b$ _____

11. $4.25 = y + 3.8$ _____   **12.** $27 = 4 + b$ _____

Algebra

Solving Equations by Multiplication

Except for the period from 1901 to 1910, when the House of Saxe-Coburg-Gotha was in power, three royal families have ruled Great Britain since 1660. Name these three "houses."

To solve:
1. Work each exercise.
2. Find the first digit of each answer to the left of the answer box. Find the second digit above the answer box.
3. Write the letter of the exercise in the box at the intersection of the row and column.

Example: A. Solve: $\frac{x}{2} = 12$

Solution: $x = 24$ Write A at the intersection of 2 and 4.

Solve.

N. $\frac{y}{4} = 13$; $y =$ _____

T. $\frac{c}{3} = 7$; $c =$ _____

T. $\frac{f}{0.7} = 40$; $f =$ _____

I. $54 = \frac{2}{3}m$; $m =$ _____

U. $\frac{n}{5} = 4.4$; $n =$ _____

D. $\frac{-3}{4r} = -63$; $r =$ _____

N. $\frac{x}{40} = 2.05$; $x =$ _____

H. $-5 = \frac{a}{-10}$; $a =$ _____

R. $\frac{c}{4} = 6\frac{1}{4}$; $c =$ _____

S. $\frac{n}{15} = \frac{4}{3}$; $n =$ _____

S. $\frac{z}{17} = 5$; $z =$ _____

V. $27\frac{1}{2} = \frac{d}{2}$; $d =$ _____

R. $\frac{h}{-59} = -1$; $h =$ _____

A. $\frac{k}{-3} = -17$; $k =$ _____

E. $9\frac{2}{3} = \frac{p}{6}$; $p =$ _____

R. $1 = \frac{h}{89}$; $h =$ _____

O. $66 = \frac{11}{9}y$; $y =$ _____

O. $\frac{b}{5} = 17.6$; $b =$ _____

W. $\frac{f}{2.5} = 32$; $f =$ _____

	0	1	2	4	5	8	9
2				A			
5							
8							

Algebra

Solving Equations by Division

What distinction do the sheepherders' houses in Baruduksun, Tibet, hold?

To solve:
1. Work each exercise.
2. Find each answer below.
3. Write the letter of the exercise above the answer.

Example: **L.** Solve: $3x = 6$

Solution: $x = 2$ Write L above 2.

Solve.

E. $4m = 20$; $m =$ _____   **I.** $7y = 56$; $y =$ _____   **G.** $6z = 54$; $z =$ _____

E. $12b = 132$; $b =$ _____   **U.** $0 = 14m$; $m =$ _____   **A.** $10n = 6$; $n =$ _____

S. $\frac{1}{2}z = 14$; $z =$ _____   **N.** $8 = 8x$; $x =$ _____   **I.** $24k = 36$; $k =$ _____

I. $175 = 25a$; $a =$ _____   **H.** $-12 = 4c =$ _____   **D.** $19r = 3.04$; $r =$ _____

B. $-7k = 63$; $k =$ _____   **N.** $24t = 288$; $t =$ _____   **D.** $\frac{3}{8}y = -9$; $y =$ _____

T. $-x = 1$; $x =$ _____   **H.** $35r = 28$; $r =$ _____   **S.** $3 = 0.05g$; $g =$ _____

T. $2.65k = 15.9$; $k =$ _____   **B.** $-19y = 95$; $y =$ _____   **I.** $3\frac{1}{7}n = 1$; $n =$ _____

I. $-20c = 50$; $c =$ _____   **G.** $\frac{1}{9}p = 1\frac{2}{3}$; $p =$ _____   **H.** $-m = 2$; $m =$ _____

___ ___ ___ ___ ___ ___ ___
-2 -2.5 15 -3 5 60 -1

___ ___ ___ ___ ___ ___ ___ ___ ___
$\frac{7}{22}$ 12 $\frac{4}{5}$ $\frac{3}{5}$ -5 1.5 6 11 -24

___ ___ ___ L ___ ___ ___ ___ ___ IN THE WORLD
-9 0 7 2 0.16 8 1 9 28

Algebra

Solving Equations Using Two Operations

On December 23, 1944, U.S. General Anthony McAuliffe sent a famous one-word reply to the German commander who ordered the surrender of McAuliffe's 101st Airborne Division. What was it?

To solve:

1. Work each exercise.
2. Find the digits of each answer on the corresponding number line. Cross out the letter that matches each digit.
3. Transfer the letters that are not crossed out, in order, to the answer below.

Example: **1.** Solve: $2x + 5 = 13$

Solution: $x = 4$ On number line I, cross out the letter matching the number 4.

Solve.

2. $2y + 5 = 57; y =$ _____

3. $44 = 4a - 20; a =$ _____

4. $6c - 15 = 153; c =$ _____

5. $\frac{x}{3} - 5 = 25; x =$ _____

6. $119 = 10y - 3y; y =$ _____

Exercises 1–6

7. $2x + 2x = 160; x =$ _____

8. $2n - 0.5n = 45; n =$ _____

9. $\frac{1}{4}d - 17 = 0; d =$ _____

10. $20 = \frac{1}{6}m + 4; m =$ _____

11. $4x - 3x = 29; x =$ _____

12. $0.2x - 22 = 25; x =$ _____

Exercises 7–12

II. R T E A L P M S H C
 0 1 2 3 4 5 6 7 8 9

___ ___ ___ ___
line line line line
 I   I   II   II

Algebra

Solving Inequalities

Inequalities

To solve an inequality, you must find the numbers that make the inequality a true statement. When you solve an inequality, you can use the same properties that you use when solving an equation, with one exception: If you are multiplying or dividing both sides of the inequality by a negative number, you must reverse the order of the inequality.

Example: Solve the inequality $-5n < -20$.

Solution: $-5n < -20$

$\dfrac{-5n}{-5} > \dfrac{-20}{-5}$ Reverse the order of the inequality when dividing by a negative number.

$n > 4$

Write an inequality using symbols for each statement. Then solve the inequality.

1. The sum of a number and 2 is less than 10.

_____

2. 5 less than a number is greater than 8.

_____

3. The product of -3 and a number is greater than 30.

_____

4. $\frac{3}{4}$ of a number is less than -6.

_____

5. The sum of -3 and 4 times a number is greater than 5.

_____

6. If -2 is added to one-half of a number, the sum is less than 4.

_____

7. The product of -5 and a number is greater than or equal to 30.

_____

8. The product of 3 and a number added to 10 is less than or equal to 16.

_____

9. 3 less than a number is less than or equal to 21.

_____

10. 10 less than one third of a number is not equal to 2.

_____

Algebra

Estimation/Mental Math

To evaluate a mathematical or algebraic expression, replace the variables with
the given numerical values and apply the rules for order of operations.

Example: Evaluate $(a - b) \times c$.   **Solution:** $(a - b) \times c$
             Let $a = 4$, $b = 3$, and $c = 2$. $(4 - 3) \times 2 = 1 \times 2 = 2$

Mentally find the value when $a = 5$, $b = 4$, and $c = 6$.

1. $6a + 3$ _____   **2.** $8b - 24$ _____   **3.** $a + (b - c)$ _____

Mentally solve for the variable.

4. $t - 43 = 10$ _____   **5.** $55 + x = 100$ _____   **6.** $\frac{x}{3} = 4$ _____

7. $8s = 96$ _____   **8.** $5b - 3 = 12$ _____   **9.** $4n + 60 = 0$ _____

10. $8y + 5 = 37$ _____   **11.** $\frac{y}{7} + 4 = 10$ _____   **12.** $\frac{s - 4}{6} = 8$ _____

13. $\frac{5}{6}n = 40$ _____   **14.** $-6m = 72$ _____   **15.** $-a = -20$ _____

16. $-96 = -6c$ _____   **17.** $-36t = -12$ _____   **18.** $\frac{s}{5} = -4$ _____

19. $7r - 12 = 37$ _____   **20.** $\frac{8}{5}z = \frac{7}{25}$ _____   **21.** $d + d = \frac{5}{6}$ _____

Mentally find the value.

22. s when $p = 28$. Formula: $p = 4s$ _____

23. e when $p = 53$ and $b = 15$. Formula: $p = b + 2e$ _____

24. a when $d = 32$ and $t = 4$. Formula: $d = \frac{1}{2} at^2$ _____

In solving inequalities, the order remains the same when you add or subtract
a positive or negative number from both sides.
The order of the inequality stays the same when you multiply or divide both sides by a
positive number. The order reverses when you multiply or divide by a negative number.

Mentally solve each inequality. Graph the solution set on a number line.

25. $x + 5 < 6$ _____

26. $2x > 8$ _____

27. $3p - 1 > 8$ _____

28. $-2x + 4 \leq 12$ _____

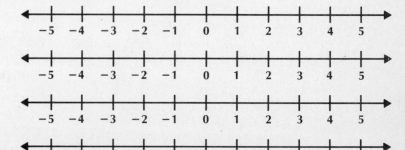

Algebra

Calculator

Solve each equation using a calculator.

1. $x + 97.34 = 183.5$ _____

2. $b - 62.1 = 859.3$ _____ ____

3. $A - 173{,}326.5 = 8{,}324.4$ _____

4. $W \div 8 = 421.8$ _____

5. $157.43\%y = 488{,}384.38$ _____

6. $0.3\%Z = 1.8$ _____

7. $882{,}663.04 \div x = 325.36$ _____

8. $16(x + 2) = 42$ _____

Use a calculator to evaluate each expression.
$a = 43.6$; $b = 4.76$; $c = 7.5$; $d = 82.63$

9. $a + b + c$ _____

10. $cd - ab$ _____

11. $\frac{a}{b} - \frac{d}{c}$ _____

12. $ab + d - c$ _____

13. $(2a + 7b) \div d$ _____

14. $12c - 2b - 12d$ _____

Solve.

15. $4.9m = 34.3$ _____

16. $p - 12.7 = 3.2$ _____

17. $x + 2.7 = 9\frac{1}{4}$ _____

18. $\frac{4}{11}x = 64$ _____

19. $\frac{d}{1.4} - 0.7 = 3.6$ _____

20. $\frac{m}{7} - 21 = 0$ _____

21. $5r - 45 = 350$ _____

22. $0.88c + 1.75 = 3.51$ _____

Solve. Use the formula $d = rt$.

23. A jet plane travels at a rate of 598 mi/h. At that rate, how far does the plane travel in 7.45

hours? _____

24. In $9\frac{1}{2}$ hours a train travels a distance of 785 miles. Find the rate of the train (to the nearest tenth).

_____

Solve each inequality.

25. $\frac{b}{25} > 340$ _____

26. $-24x < 7{,}872$ _____

27. Find the value of l when $p = 220$ and $w = 28$. Formula: $l = \frac{p}{2} - w$ _____

Locating Points in the Number Plane

Coordinate Confusion

What are the coordinates of the point in the number plane below?

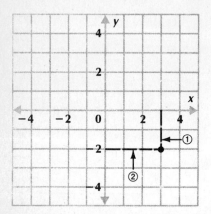

(3,−2)

1. Remember, the x-axis is horizontal.
Draw a perpendicular line from the point to the x-axis.
The line intersects the x-axis at 3.
The first component is 3.

2. Remember, the y-axis is vertical.
Draw a perpendicular line from the point to the y-axis.
The line intersects the y-axis at −2.
The second component is −2.

3. Write the component for the x-axis
followed by a comma and the
component for the y-axis.
Enclose the coordinates in parentheses.

Choose the coordinates of each indicated point.

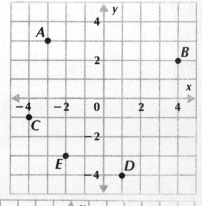

1. A   **a.** (3,−3)   **b.** (−3,3)   **c.** (3,3)   _____

2. B   **a.** (4,2)   **b.** (2,4)   **c.** (−4,2)   _____

3. C   **a.** (4,−1)   **b.** (−1,−4)   **c.** (−4,−1)   _____

4. D   **a.** (1,−4)   **b.** (−4,1)   **c.** (−4,−1)   _____

5. E   **a.** (−3,−2)   **b.** (−2,3)   **c.** (−2,−3)   _____

Write the coordinates of each indicated point.

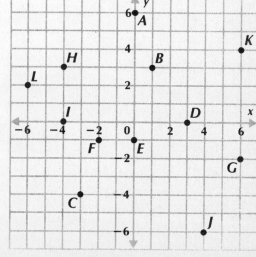

6. A _____   7. B _____

8. C _____   9. D _____

10. E _____   11. F _____

12. G _____   13. H _____

14. I _____   15. J _____

16. K _____   17. L _____

Coordinate Graphing

Plotting Points in the Number Plane

What was the name of the woman who became George Washington's wife, the first "First Lady" of the United States?

To solve:
1. For each exercise, find the letter of the point at the position indicated by the given coordinates.
2. Write the letter above the number of the exercise below.

Example: **1.** Find the point with coordinates (2,4).

Solution: point A Write A above 1.

Find the points that have the following coordinates.

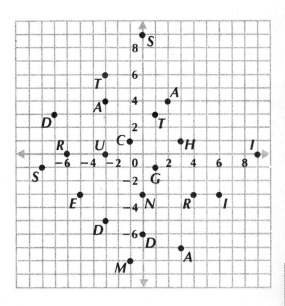

2. (−6,0) _____   **3.** (3,1) _____

4. (−8,−1) _____   **5.** (6,−3) _____

6. (−3,4) _____   **7.** (−5,−3) _____

8. (1,3) _____   **9.** (−1,−8) _____

10. (3,−7) _____   **11.** (0,−6) _____

12. (0, −3) _____   **13.** (9,0) _____

14. (1,−1) _____   **15.** (−3,6) _____

16. (4,−3) _____   **17.** (−3,−5) _____

18. (−7,3) _____   **19.** (−3,0) _____

20. (0,9) _____   **21.** (−1,1) _____

___ ___ ___ ___ ___ ___   ___ A ___ ___ ___ ___ ___ ___ ___
 9   10   2   8   3   6   18   1   12 11 16   5   17 14   7

___ ___ ___ ___ ___ ___
21 19   4   15 13 20

Coordinate Graphing

NAME _____ CLASS _____ DATE _____

Plotting Points in the Number Plane

Translating Polygons

You can slide, or *translate*, △RST to get △R'S'T' by adding 6 to the first coordinate of each vertex. The rule for the translation is $(x,y) \to (x + 6,y)$.

R: $(-4,1) \to (2,1)$
S: $(-2,1) \to (4,1)$
T: $(-3,4) \to (3,4)$

Use the rules below to translate △RST to other locations on the grid. Draw each translation on the grid with a different color pencil.

1. $(x,y) \to (x,y - 4)$

2. $(x,y) \to (x + 3,y)$

3. $(x,y) \to (x + 9,y + 2)$

4. $(x,y) \to (x + 8,y - 6)$

Write the coordinates for each vertex in quadrilateral *ABCD*.

5. A _____

6. B _____

7. C _____

8. D _____

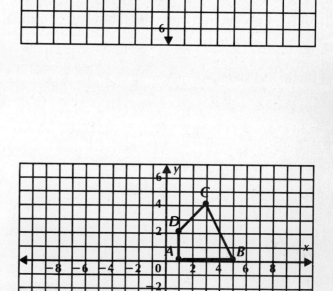

Use the rules below to translate quadrilateral *ABCD* to other locations on the grid. Draw each translation on the grid with a different color pencil.

9. $(x,y) \to (x - 5,y)$

10. $(x,y) \to (x,y - 6)$

11. $(x,y) \to (x + 5,y - 5)$

12. $(x,y) \to (x - 4,y - 4)$

Coordinate Graphing

Graphing an Equation in the Number Plane

Developing a Table of Values

Draw the graph of $y = 2x$. First make a table of solutions of the equation. Then plot those points on a graph.

x	$y = 2x$	y	(x,y)
0	$y = 2 (0)$	0	$(0,0)$
1	$y = 2 (1)$	2	$(1,2)$
2	$y = 2 (2)$	4	$(2,4)$

Select values for x and substitute them for x in the equation. Start with $x = 0$.
$y = 2x = 2(0) = 0$
Then use the x and y values to write the ordered pair.
Substitute 1 for x. Solve for y.
Substitute 2 for x. Solve for y.

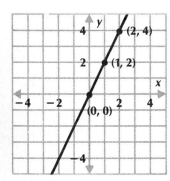

Now, plot the three ordered pairs from the table in a number plane.
Join the points with a line.
This is the graph of $y = 2x$.

Complete each table of values.

1. $x - y = 3$

x	y
3	
4	
5	

2. $6x = -3y$

x	y
0	
1	
2	

3. $4y = -16$

x	y
-2	
0	
2	

Develop a table of values, then draw the graph for each equation.

4. $x = y + 3$

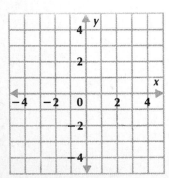

5. $3x = 5y$

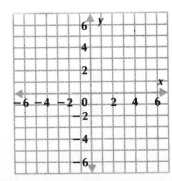

6. $4y = 12$

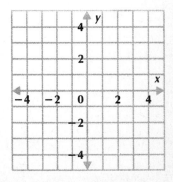

Coordinate Graphing

Graphing an Equation in the Number Plane

Graphing

For each equation below, complete a table of values. Then graph the four equations on the grid at the right. Write the equation on each line.

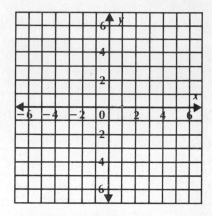

1. $y = x$

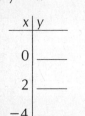

x	y
0	___
2	___
−4	___

2. $y = x + 3$

x	y
0	___
−2	___
1	___

3. $y = 2x$

x	y
0	___
−1	___
2	___

4. $y = x - 4$

x	y
5	___
2	___
0	___

For each equation below, complete a table of values. Then graph the three equations on the grid at the right. Write the equation on each line.

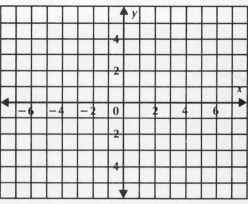

5. $y = -3x + 2$

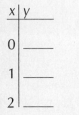

x	y
0	___
1	___
2	___

6. $y = x + 3$

x	y
0	___
−2	___
1	___

7. $y = \frac{1}{3}x - 1$

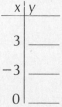

x	y
3	___
−3	___
0	___

Coordinate Graphing

Graphing an Equation in the Number Plane

Some geologists theorize that all of the earth's continents may once have been joined together in a single land mass. What is the name they have given to this hypothetical "super-continent"?

To solve:
1. Decide which of the given graphs is the graph of each equation.
2. Write the letter of the graph above the number of the exercise below.

Example: **1.** Which of the given graphs is the graph of $y = x$?

Solution: graph A Write A above 1.

Which graph is the graph of each equation?

2. $y = x + 3$ _____

3. $y = x - 5$ _____

4. $x = y - 5$ _____

5. $x + y = 0$ _____

6. $y = -3$ _____

7. $y = 2x$ _____

8. $x = -3$ _____

9. $y = 0$ _____

10. $x = 0$ _____

11. $y = 3$ _____

12. $5y = -15x$ _____

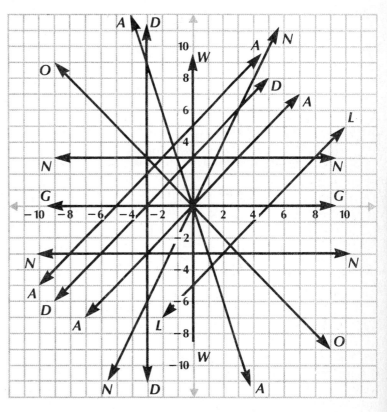

__	__	__	__	__	A	__	__	__	__	__	__
9	5	7	2	10	1	6	4	3	12	11	8

Coordinate Graphing

Review

1. Write the ordered pair of numbers that has 3 as the first component and −1 as the second component. _____

What are the coordinates of each point?

2. Point K _____

3. Point L _____

4. Point M _____

5. Point N _____

6. Point O _____

7. Point P _____

8. Point Q _____

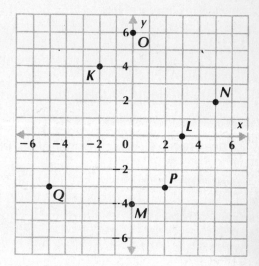

On graph paper, draw axes and plot points with the following coordinates.

9. R (2,−5)   10. S (−3,4)   11. T (0,6)   12. U (−1,−7)

13. V (4,0)   14. W (−5,−5)   15. X (7,1)   16. Y (−2,3)

Draw the graph of each of the following equations.

17. $y = -2x + 1$

18. $x = y + 3$

19. $-6y = 3x$

20. $x = 2$

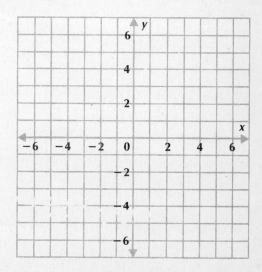

Coordinate Graphing

▨▨ ANSWERS ▨▨

Unit 1 Whole Numbers

Worksheet 1   **1.** seven hundred four   **2.** five thousand, thirty-eight   **3.** thirty-six thousand, four hundred twelve   **4.** three hundred thousand   **5.** two million, twenty   **6.** seven hundred million, three hundred twenty-one thousand, fifteen

Worksheet 2   **1.** 2,604,000   **2.** correct   **3.** 803,000,037   **4.** 915,000,000,000   **5.** 6,032   **6.** 8,002   **7.** 73,000   **8.** 50,000,291   **9.** 8,025,000

Worksheet 3   **1.** 8,000   **2.** 680,500   **3.** 1,000,000,000   **4.** 900   **5.** 280,500,000   **6.** 600,700   **7.** 1,200   **8.** 3,300   **9.** 704   **10.** 50,000   **11.** 9,000,500,721   **12.** 400,016   **13.** 20,090,006   **14.** 300,900,000   **15.** 50,048   **16.** 800,006,000   **17.** 7,000,000,000,000   **18.** 503   **19.** 4,008   **20.** 25,023

Worksheet 4   **2.** 40   **3.** 20   **4.** 120   **5.** 800   **6.** 4,400   **7.** 6,100   **8.** 7,000   **9.** 63,000   **10.** 51,000   **11.** 240,000   **12.** 840,000   **13.** 1,400,000   **14.** 4,200,000
ROBINSON CRUSOE

Worksheet 5   **1.** est., 70; sum, 65   **2.** est., 80; sum, 77   **3.** est., 150; sum, 146   **4.** est., 160; sum, 158   **5.** est., 600; sum, 615   **6.** est., 9,000; sum, 8,403   **7.** est., 1,400; sum, 1,419   **8.** est., 16,000, sum, 16,607   **9.** est., 40,000; sum, 41,507

Worksheet 6   **1.** est., 40; diff., 37   **2.** est., 40; diff., 44   **3.** est., 20; diff., 24   **4.** est., 290, diff., 288   **5.** est., 200; diff., 219   **6.** est., 200; diff., 181   **7.** est., 20,000; diff., 19,178   **8.** est., 30,000; diff., 30,509

Worksheet 7   **1.** 42   **2.** 64   **3.** 54   **4.** 20   **5.** 5   **6.** 35   **7.** 223   **8.** 285   **9.** 420   **10.** 267   **11.** 59   **12.** 518   **13.** 2,875   **14.** 3,624   **15.** 2,075   **16.** 2,159   **17.** 23,331   **18.** 25,796   **19.** 38,147   **20.** 613,619; THE EROICA

Worksheet 8   **1.** b   **2.** a   **3.** c   **4.** c   **5.** b   **6.** est., 240, prod., 232   **7.** est., 560; prod., 553   **8.** est., 400; prod., 310   **9.** est., 2,100; prod., 2,106   **10.** est., 1,500; prod., 1,521   **11.** est., 4,800; prod., 4,960

Worksheet 9   **A.** 1,005   **E.** 12,892   **N.** 274,575   **L.** 28,700   **D.** 850   **L.** 33,957   **E.** 1,570,578   **G.** 194,971   **O.** 116,162   **H.** 5,362,811   **R.** 8,361,954   **N.** 579,600   **I.** 540,000   **N.** 205,530   **M.** 448,305   **C.** 25,810,972   **T.** 51,732   **O.** 2,262   **W.** 675,514   **R.** $n = 4,704$
WILHELM CONRAD ROENTGEN

Worksheet 10   **1.** b   **2.** c   **3.** b   **4.** a   **5.** 68   **6.** 509   **7.** 207   **8.** 4,071   **9.** 5,603   **10.** 170   **11.** 826   **12.** 408

Worksheet 11   **S.** 12   **I.** 78   **R.** 64   **N.** 122   **E.** 695   **P.** 833   **M.** 2,145   **O.** 5,903   **C.** 7,029   **A.** 6,026   **F.** 8,252   **O.** 2,506   **E.** 3,575   **M.** 8,123   **R.** 4,188
JAMES FENIMORE COOPER

Worksheet 12   **1.** true   **2.** false   **3.** false   **4.** true   **5.** 27   **6.** 73 R6   **7.** 309 R18   **8.** 7,005   **9.** 571 R17   **10.** 609 R71

Worksheet 13   **2.** 83   **3.** 19   **4.** 128   **5.** 214   **6.** 1,321   **7.** 2,416   **8.** 3   **9.** 18   **10.** 465   **11.** 806
"FIRST IN WAR, FIRST IN PEACE, AND FIRST IN THE HEARTS OF HIS COUNTRYMEN"

Worksheet 14   **1. a.** 1, 2, 4, 8, 16   **b.** 1, 2, 3, 4, 6, 8, 12, 24   **c.** 1, 2, 4, 8   **2. a.** 1, 3, 9, 27, 81   **b.** 1, 3, 9, 11, 33, 99   **c.** 1, 3, 9   **3.** 2   **4.** 25   **5.** 3   **6.** 72

Worksheet 15   **2.** 2   **3.** 15   **4.** 3   **5.** 5   **6.** 4   **7.** 16   **8.** 14   **9.** 10   **10.** 12   **11.** 20   **12.** 13   **13.** 1
BRISTLECONE PINE TREE OF CALIFORNIA

Worksheet 16 **1.** b **2.** b **3.** a **4. a.** 0, 12, 24, 36, 48, 60 **b.** 0, 15, 30, 45, 60, 75; LCM: 60 **5. a.** 0, 9, 18, 27, 36, 45 **b.** 0, 6, 12, 18, 24, 30; LCM: 18 **6.** 36 **7.** 45 **8.** 63 **9.** 30

Worksheet 17 **1.** 42 **2.** 88 **3.** 104 **4.** 112 **5.** 225 **6.** 63 **7.** 0, 6, 12, 18 **8.** 0, 8, 16, 24 **9.** 0, 24, 48, 72 **10.** 0, 7, 14, 21 **11.** 0, 9, 18, 27 **12.** 0, 13, 26, 39 **13.** 10, 20, 30 **14.** 14, 28, 42 **15.** 24, 48, 72 **16.** 24, 48, 72 **17.** 21, 42, 63 **18.** 20, 40, 60 **19.** 15 **20.** 75 **21.** 60 **22.** 30 **23.** 60 **24.** 24 **25.** 24 **26.** 96 **27.** 24 **28.** 14 **29.** 153 **30.** 140

Worksheet 18 **1.** 36 × 4 **2.** 24 ÷ 4 **3.** 55 **4.** 80 **5.** 61 **6.** 60 **7.** 14 **8.** 83,790 **9.** 700 **10.** 110 **11.** 20; 9,345 **12.** 28; 3,491 **13.** 700,000 **14.** 400,000 **15.** 3,200,000 **16.** 2,000

Worksheet 19 **1.** Twenty thousand, four hundred ninety-seven **2.** Six hundred eighty-seven million, five hundred two thousand **3.** Three million, four hundred sixty thousand, five **4.** 32,618,009,012 **5.** 443,075,000 **6.** 740 **7.** 587,000 **8.** 8,400,000 **9.** 69,835 **10.** 1,799 **11.** 6,592 **12.** 22,877 **13.** 123,722 **14.** 23,625 **15.** 198,645 **16.** 14,628 **17.** 50,008 **18.** 459 **19.** 364 **20.** 1, 2, 5, 10, 25, 50 **21.** 18

Unit 2 Decimals

Worksheet 20 **1.** ten-thousandths **2.** hundred-thousandths **3.** thousandths **4.** millionths **5.** eight and three tenths **6.** one and seven tenths **7.** nine hundredths **8.** thirty-seven and fifty-four hundredths **9.** two hundred sixteen and seven thousandths **10.** thirteen and six hundred twenty-one thousandths **11.** one and five thousand two hundred ninety-one ten-thousandths **12.** four and two thousand fifty-six hundred-thousandths

Worksheet 21 **1.** five tenths **2.** three thousandths **3.** three and eighty-seven thousandths **4.** forty-nine hundredths **5.** seven hundred-thousandths **6.** seventy-five hundredths **7.** six hundredths **8.** eight and thirty-seven hundredths **9.** four hundred-thousandths **10.** three and five tenths **11.** two millionths **12.** eight hundredths **13.** two and eight tenths **14.** fifty-one ten-thousandths **15.** one ten-thousandth **16.** thirty-five **17.** seventeen and twenty-eight thousandths **18.** six ten-thousandths **19.** three hundred ninety-six thousandths **20.** fifteen thousandths **21.** one and six hundred four thousandths **22.** five and forty-eight hundredths

Worksheet 22 **1.** 0.355 **2.** correct **3.** 0.0022 **4.** correct **5.** 1.00007 **6.** 17.5 **7.** 0.034 **8.** 600.085 **9.** 0.0105 **10.** 410.1005 **11.** 0.00086 **12.** 0.000526

Worksheet 23 **1.** c **2.** a **3.** d **4.** 24.90 **5.** 0.08 **6.** 266.00 **7.** 0.0854 **8.** 2.8451 **9.** 0.3480

Worksheet 24 **1.** 232; between 229 and 233 **2.** 844; between 842 and 846 **3.** 338; between 337 and 341 **4.** 157; between 157 and 161 **5.** yes **6.** yes **7.** $3; between $1 and $6; the usual method of rounding

Worksheet 25 **1.** 17.953 **2.** 0.8 **3.** 31.72 **4.** 0.55 **5.** 0.006 **6.** 3.98 **7.** 0.088 **8.** 0.020019 **9.** 2.3, 2.03, 0.320, 0.23, 0.023 **10.** 34, 1.4, 0.42, 0.308 **11.** 2.9, 1.802, 0.9203, 0.88 **12.** 0.098, 0.918, 0.98, 1.98 **13.** 2.09, 2.18, 2.19, 2.9 **14.** 9.98, 23.87, 84.399, 311.88, 412.802

Worksheet 26 **1.** b **2.** a **3.** a **4.** 47.38 **5.** 1,621.73 **6.** 386.76 **7.** 14.029

Worksheet 27 **1.** 0.9 **2.** 2.1 **3.** 7.9 **4.** 0.17 **5.** 7.80 **6.** 21.25 **7.** 19.52 **8.** 21.88 **9.** 18.514 **10.** 138.05 **11.** 168.05 **12.** 92.361 GUERNICA

Answers

Worksheet 28   **1.** b   **2.** a   **3.** b   **4.** c   **5.** est., 2; diff., 1.89   **6.** est., 3; diff., 2.65   **7.** est., 7; diff., 6.865   **8.** est., 14; diff., 14.575   **9.** est., 21; diff., 21.388   **10.** est., 30; diff., 30.287   **11.** est., $329; diff., $328.84   **12.** est., $8; diff., $7.92

Worksheet 29   **1.** 0.068   **2.** 0.00258   **3.** 0.0412   **4.** 0.1150   **5.** b   **6.** c   **7.** a   **8.** b   **9.** est., 0.06; prod., 0.06   **10.** est., 0.07; prod., 0.0735   **11.** est., 0.16; diff., 0.128   **12.** est., 2.1; prod., 1.84064

Worksheet 30   **1.** 2.8   **2.** 38.88   **3.** 29.946   **4.** 7.4178   **5.** 25.5   **6.** 1.12   **7.** 0.48   **8.** 0.091   **9.** 0.0096   **10.** 1,026   **11.** 0.4   **12.** 0.03   **13.** 0.216   **14.** 0.056   **15.** 1.12   **16.** 0.0416   **17.** 0.588   **18.** 0.000018   **19.** 0.0246   **20.** 32.98408   **21.** 0.000018   **22.** $8.68   **23.** $79.17   **24.** $7.70   **25.** 4.8   **26.** 0.225   **27.** 25.5   **28.** a   **29.** $n = 0.021$

Worksheet 31   **1.** 260   **2.** 200   **3.** 2   **4.** 78   **5.** 3.6   **6.** 0.5   **7.** 0.062   **8.** 5,387.11   **9.** 3,800   **10.** 17,000   **11.** 50   **12.** 960   **13.** 48   **14.** 0.91   **15.** 3   **16.** 28,611.4   **17.** 45,000   **18.** 400,000   **19.** 500   **20.** 12,400   **21.** 780   **22.** 7.1   **23.** 91   **24.** 1,428,092   **25.** 254,000   **26.** 3,800,000   **27.** 45,200,000   **28.** 804,630   **29.** 47   **30.** 6,903,100

Worksheet 32   **1.** 0.055   **2.** 0.25   **3.** 0.036   **4.** 0.138   **5.** 5.89   **6.** 13.5   **7.** 0.0428   **8.** 0.075   **9.** est., 0.2; quo., 0.2   **10.** est., 0.6; quo., 0.635   **11.** est., 7; quo., 6.8   **12.** est., 0.5; quo., 0.5   **13.** est., 0.01; quo., 0.02   **14.** est., 6; quo., 6.36

Worksheet 33   **1.** b   **2.** c   **3.** c   **4.** a   **5.** 0.03   **6.** 0.011   **7.** 0.06   **8.** 0.002

Worksheet 34   **T.** 0.778   **A.** 30   **H.** 477   **O.** 507.14   **I.** 0.036   **S.** 22.5   **L.** 270   **R.** 381   **N.** 6.22   **V.** 0.017   **A.** 79.8   **A.** 75   **K.** 123   **N.** 0.45   **V.** 6.8   VALENTINA TERESHKOVA

Worksheet 35   **1.** b   **2.** b   **3.** a   **4.** 4.5   **5.** 31.23   **6.** 0.09   **7.** 0.003   **8.** 70.2   **9.** 0.0475   **10.** 0.867   **11.** 0.18   **12.** 0.45   **13.** 3.832   **14.** 0.0008   **15.** 0.00328   **16.** 0.602   **17.** 0.01835   **18.** 5.9706   **19.** 0.009573   **20.** 0.35   **21.** 4.5   **22.** 0.0068   **23.** 0.000921   **24.** 0.023

Worksheet 36   **1.** 67   **2.** 9   **3.** 15   **4.** 3   **5.** 30.1   **6.** 5.4   **7.** 2.2   **8.** 0.1   **9.** 60   **10.** 5   **11.** 15   **12.** 0.4   **13.** 24   **14.** 10   **15.** 7   **16.** 4   **17.** 4   **18.** 5   **19.** 7.2   **20.** 6.8   **21.** 54   **22.** 400   **23.** 5,000   **24.** 40,000   **25.** 6,500   **26.** 65,000   **27.** 8.6   **28.** 86   **29.** 860   **30.** 8,600   **31.** 2   **32.** 20   **33.** 4   **34.** 40   **35. a.** $110 **b.** $10   **36.** $492   **37.** yes

Worksheet 37   **1.** <   **2.** =   **3.** >   **4.** <   **5.** <   **6.** <   **7.** <   **8.** >   **9.** <   **10.** <   **11.** =   **12.** >   **13.** <   **14.** <   **15.** <   **16.** >   **17.** 2.08   **18.** 0.000494   **19.** 19.35   **20.** 0.000256   **21.** 13.6   **22.** 0.999   **23.** 170   **24.** 471.9   **25.** 0.168   **26.** 0.2268   **27.** 0.9765   **28.** 5.112   **29.** 123.5   **30.** 0.88682   **31.** 284.55   **32.** 7,000   **33.** 25.4   **34.** 32.02   **35.** 18.61   **36.** 2.2   **37.** 14   **38.** 250   **39.** 2.2   **40.** 19.93

Worksheet 38   **1.** b   **2.** a   **3.** b   **4.** $\frac{6}{10}$ **5.** $\frac{21}{30}$ **6.** $\frac{5}{11}$ **7.** $\frac{2}{3}$ **8.** $\frac{23}{27}$ **9.** $\frac{3}{7}$

Worksheet 39   **2.** $\frac{3}{4}$ **3.** $\frac{5}{16}$ **4.** $\frac{4}{5}$ **5.** $\frac{5}{8}$ **6.** $\frac{3}{5}$ **7.** $\frac{11}{15}$ **8.** $\frac{2}{3}$ **9.** $\frac{9}{10}$ **10.** $\frac{13}{15}$ **11.** $\frac{9}{16}$ **12.** $\frac{1}{4}$ **13.** $\frac{9}{10}$ **14.** 15   **15.** 14   **16.** 14

"IT IS A FAR, FAR BETTER REST THAT I GO TO THAN I HAVE EVER KNOWN"

Worksheet 40   **1.** 1, 2, 3, 4, 6, 9, 12, 18, 36; 1, 2, 3, 4, 6, 8, 12, 16, 24, 48; 12   **2.** 1, 2, 3, 6, 7, 14, 21, 42; 1, 7, 11, 77; 7   **3.** 1, 2, 17, 34; 1, 5, 17, 85; 17   **4.** 1, 3, 5, 9, 15, 45; 1, 2, 3, 4, 5, 6, 8, 10, 12, 15, 20, 24, 30, 40, 60, 120; 15   **5.** 13   **6.** 16   **7.** 9   **8.** 18   **9.** $\frac{7}{8}$ **10.** $\frac{2}{3}$ **11.** $\frac{4}{9}$ **12.** $\frac{1}{4}$ **13.** $\frac{1}{6}$ **14.** $\frac{1}{3}$

Worksheet 41 1. $\frac{2}{5}$ 2. $\frac{9}{28}$ 3. $\frac{42}{53}$ 4. $\frac{15}{22}$ 5. $\frac{13}{47}$ 6. $\frac{16}{17}$ 7. $\frac{7}{38}$ 8. $\frac{21}{32}$ 9. $\frac{12}{19}$ 10. $\frac{8}{75}$ 11. $\frac{36}{53}$ 12. $\frac{24}{25}$

Worksheet 42 1. a 2. b 3. a 4. 4 5. $1\frac{7}{11}$ 6. $1\frac{7}{9}$ 7. $6\frac{1}{4}$ 8. $3\frac{1}{4}$ 9. $3\frac{1}{3}$ 10. $2\frac{1}{2}$ 11. $6\frac{2}{5}$ 12. $7\frac{3}{7}$ 13. 16 14. $12\frac{3}{4}$ 15. $6\frac{2}{3}$ 16. $35\frac{1}{4}$ 17. $10\frac{1}{8}$ 18. $5\frac{1}{2}$

Worksheet 43 2. 2 3. $1\frac{3}{8}$ 4. $4\frac{1}{2}$ 5. $2\frac{1}{4}$ 6. $5\frac{5}{8}$ 7. $6\frac{5}{8}$ 8. $6\frac{7}{8}$ 9. $4\frac{1}{2}$ 10. $2\frac{1}{4}$ 11. $1\frac{1}{8}$ 12. $2\frac{3}{4}$ 13. $6\frac{3}{8}$ 14. 2 15. $1\frac{3}{8}$ 16. $2\frac{1}{4}$ 17. $2\frac{3}{4}$ 18. $4\frac{1}{2}$ 19. $6\frac{3}{8}$ 20. $2\frac{1}{4}$ 21. $5\frac{5}{8}$ 22. $4\frac{5}{8}$ 23. 2 24. $4\frac{1}{2}$ 25. $6\frac{7}{8}$ 26. $1\frac{3}{8}$ 27. $1\frac{3}{8}$ 28. $3\frac{3}{4}$ 29. $4\frac{1}{2}$ 30. $6\frac{3}{8}$ 31. $2\frac{1}{4}$ 32. $1\frac{1}{4}$ 33. $2\frac{3}{4}$

THE SIXTH SICK SHEIK'S SIXTH SHEEP'S SICK

Worksheet 44 A. $\frac{7}{8}$ Y. $\frac{5}{64}$ Z. $\frac{7}{16}$ T. $\frac{5}{32}$ O. $\frac{7}{32}$ B. $\frac{5}{8}$ A. $\frac{7}{13}$ R. $\frac{5}{16}$ M. $\frac{7}{11}$ S. $\frac{7}{72}$ N. $4\frac{1}{2}$ I. $\frac{1}{4}$ N. $2\frac{7}{64}$ I. $1\frac{5}{13}$ O. $\frac{5}{6}$ H. $1\frac{5}{81}$ E. $1\frac{1}{6}$

NILE OB-IRTYSH AMAZON

Worksheet 45 1. c 2. b 3. d 4. a 5. 8; $\frac{2}{8}$, $\frac{3}{8}$ 6. 6; $\frac{3}{6}$, $\frac{5}{6}$ 7. 24; $\frac{11}{24}$, $\frac{16}{24}$ 8. 20; $\frac{7}{20}$, $\frac{16}{20}$ 9. 12; $\frac{8}{12}$, $\frac{9}{12}$ 10. 72; $\frac{32}{72}$, $\frac{27}{72}$ 11. 24; $\frac{14}{24}$, $\frac{9}{24}$ 12. 30; $\frac{15}{30}$, $\frac{20}{30}$, $\frac{18}{30}$ 13. 16; $\frac{4}{16}$, $\frac{6}{16}$, $\frac{9}{16}$ 14. 24; $\frac{16}{24}$, $\frac{6}{24}$, $\frac{15}{24}$

Worksheet 46 1. $\frac{8}{9}$; $\frac{32}{36}$, $\frac{27}{36}$, $\frac{30}{36}$, $\frac{24}{36}$ 2. $\frac{7}{8}$; $\frac{64}{80}$, $\frac{65}{80}$, $\frac{70}{80}$, $\frac{62}{80}$ 3. $\frac{7}{10}$; $\frac{45}{70}$, $\frac{34}{70}$, $\frac{35}{70}$, $\frac{49}{70}$ 4. $\frac{13}{14}$; $\frac{28}{42}$, $\frac{12}{42}$, $\frac{39}{42}$, $\frac{35}{42}$ 5. $\frac{19}{21}$; $\frac{76}{84}$, $\frac{75}{84}$, $\frac{74}{84}$, $\frac{44}{84}$ 6. $\frac{31}{32}$; $\frac{30}{96}$, $\frac{93}{96}$, $\frac{40}{96}$, $\frac{76}{96}$ 7. $\frac{5}{6}$; $\frac{20}{30}$, $\frac{24}{30}$, $\frac{6}{30}$, $\frac{25}{30}$ 8. $\frac{5}{6}$; $\frac{45}{72}$, $\frac{60}{72}$, $\frac{52}{72}$, $\frac{40}{72}$ 9. $\frac{13}{75}$; $\frac{18}{150}$, $\frac{26}{150}$, $\frac{21}{150}$, $\frac{20}{150}$ 10. $\frac{19}{22}$; $\frac{54}{66}$, $\frac{55}{66}$, $\frac{57}{66}$, $\frac{42}{66}$ 11. $\frac{12}{13}$; $\frac{46}{104}$, $\frac{96}{104}$, $\frac{28}{104}$, $\frac{91}{104}$ 12. $\frac{5}{6}$; $\frac{27}{36}$, $\frac{21}{36}$, $\frac{30}{36}$, $\frac{16}{36}$

Worksheet 47 1. c 2. a 3. b 4. a 5. b 6. c 7. 8 8. 6 9. 6 10. 20 11. 12 12. 30 13. 45 14. 52 15. 30 16. $\frac{40}{64}$ 17. $\frac{6}{12}$ 18. $\frac{9}{21}$ 19. $\frac{32}{72}$ 20. $\frac{105}{120}$ 21. $\frac{38}{150}$ 22. $\frac{105}{15}$ 23. $\frac{450}{30}$ 24. $\frac{378}{42}$

Worksheet 48 1. b 2. c 3. a 4. b 5. $1\frac{1}{4}$ 6. $\frac{5}{9}$ 7. $1\frac{3}{20}$ 8. $7\frac{6}{11}$ 9. $14\frac{2}{3}$ 10. $12\frac{9}{10}$ 11. $13\frac{13}{24}$ 12. $17\frac{39}{40}$ 13. $13\frac{7}{60}$ 14. $12\frac{11}{18}$ 15. $99\frac{32}{33}$ 16. $21\frac{11}{12}$ 17. $31\frac{7}{60}$ 18. $1\frac{7}{12}$ 19. $1\frac{3}{16}$

Worksheet 49 N. $1\frac{2}{5}$ L. $1\frac{1}{2}$ A. $1\frac{1}{6}$ T. $\frac{13}{20}$ O. $\frac{19}{24}$ A. $7\frac{2}{5}$ B. $7\frac{7}{9}$ L. $6\frac{1}{2}$ I. 6 O. $6\frac{4}{7}$ H. $1\frac{1}{12}$ O. $6\frac{5}{9}$ A. $6\frac{1}{4}$

A HOT AIR BALLOON

Worksheet 50 1. c 2. a 3. b 4. a 5. $\frac{5}{36}$ 6. $\frac{25}{48}$ 7. $\frac{1}{2}$ 8. $\frac{11}{20}$ 9. $3\frac{4}{15}$ 10. $15\frac{3}{10}$ 11. $8\frac{4}{11}$ 12. $10\frac{5}{9}$ 13. $5\frac{31}{32}$

Worksheet 51 2. $\frac{1}{2}$ 3. $\frac{3}{8}$ 4. $\frac{1}{12}$ 5. $8\frac{4}{9}$ 6. $3\frac{1}{6}$ 7. $1\frac{4}{5}$ 8. $4\frac{3}{4}$ 9. $4\frac{5}{9}$ 10. $3\frac{1}{8}$ 11. $4\frac{2}{3}$ 12. $3\frac{3}{4}$ 13. $6\frac{1}{2}$ 14. $1\frac{5}{6}$ 15. $3\frac{3}{5}$ 16. $5\frac{2}{5}$ 17. $\frac{3}{4}$ 18. $6\frac{5}{8}$ 19. $\frac{2}{9}$

ALEKSANDR SOLZHENITSYN

Worksheet 52

1. $\frac{5}{2}$ 2. $\frac{29}{8}$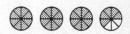

3. $\frac{9}{5}$ 4. $\frac{11}{4}$

5. $\frac{3}{2}$ 6. $\frac{11}{6}$ 7. $\frac{22}{15}$ 8. $\frac{31}{19}$ 9. $\frac{22}{3}$ 10. $\frac{79}{8}$

Worksheet 53 1. b 2. a 3. c 4. b 5. a 6. c 7. $\frac{1}{21}$ 8. $\frac{35}{48}$ 9. $4\frac{1}{2}$ 10. $6\frac{2}{5}$ 11. 3 12. $5\frac{1}{3}$

Worksheet 54 2. $\frac{6}{35}$ 3. $\frac{1}{4}$ 4. $\frac{5}{14}$ 5. $\frac{2}{3}$ 6. $6\frac{2}{3}$ 7. $1\frac{3}{4}$ 8. 6 9. $3\frac{3}{4}$ 10. $2\frac{1}{10}$ 11. 20 12. $28\frac{1}{2}$ 13. $11\frac{2}{3}$ 14. 18 15. $17\frac{1}{3}$ 16. $7\frac{1}{5}$ 17. $\frac{1}{8}$ 18. 21 19. $3\frac{1}{3}$ 20. $n = 4\frac{1}{5}$

CRESTLESS GARDENER BOWERBIRD

Answers

Worksheet 55 1. a 2. b 3. c 4. a 5. $\frac{7}{8}$ 6. $\frac{10}{13}$
7. $\frac{2}{3}$ 8. $1\frac{1}{5}$ 9. $\frac{5}{12}$ 10. $\frac{1}{9}$ 11. 10 12. 34 13. 4
14. $\frac{5}{33}$ 15. $1\frac{8}{11}$ 16. $1\frac{1}{5}$ 17. $\frac{15}{16}$ 18. $1\frac{1}{2}$

Worksheet 56 I. $2\frac{2}{15}$ E. $\frac{2}{3}$ I. 3 S. $2\frac{1}{10}$ Y. $\frac{1}{10}$
I. 27 L. $13\frac{1}{3}$ U. $\frac{1}{4}$ M. $2\frac{1}{4}$ A. 14 T. $\frac{6}{11}$ O. $\frac{4}{17}$
D. 6 A. 4 L. $\frac{1}{10}$ G. $\frac{1}{2}$ L. $\frac{14}{55}$ G. $\frac{4}{5}$ H. $17\frac{1}{2}$
C. $1\frac{1}{8}$ O. $n = 2\frac{2}{3}$
MIGUEL HIDALGO Y COSTILLA

Worksheet 57 2. $\frac{1}{5}$ 3. $\frac{3}{4}$ 4. $\frac{1}{20}$ 5. $2\frac{5}{8}$ 6. $\frac{1}{4}$
7. $\frac{7}{8}$ 8. $1\frac{1}{8}$ 9. $4\frac{1}{10}$ 10. $1\frac{5}{16}$ 11. $\frac{7}{10}$ 12. $\frac{9}{16}$
13. $1\frac{1}{16}$ 14. $2\frac{3}{10}$ 15. $8\frac{7}{16}$ 16. $2\frac{3}{4}$ 17. $\frac{3}{16}$
MATCHLESS MOUNTAIN

Worksheet 58 1. $0.\overline{4}$ 2. $5.8\overline{6}$ 3. $12.8\overline{25}$
4. $8 \times 0.\overline{1}$ 5. $58 \times 0.\overline{01}$ 6. $17 \times 0.\overline{01}$
7. $651 \times 0.\overline{001}$ 8. $7 \times 0.\overline{1}$ 9. $25 \times 0.\overline{01}$ 10. $\frac{2}{9}$
11. $\frac{2}{3}$ 12. $\frac{85}{99}$ 13. $\frac{4}{99}$ 14. $19\frac{5}{9}$ 15. $\frac{41}{333}$ 16. $2\frac{8}{9}$
17. $\frac{13}{99}$ 18. $8\frac{2}{33}$

Worksheet 59 1. 0.6 2. 0.875 3. 0.7 4. 0.25
5. 8.3 6. 3.9 7. 0.82 8. 1.04 9. 6.4 10. 18.64
11. 5.35 12. 0.22 13. 0.6875 14. 0.25 15. 1.65
16. 0.055 17. 2.125 18. 4.2 19. 1.1875 20. 6.4
21. 1.3125 22. 0.42 23. 0.625 24. 0.0127 25. 2.875

Worksheet 60 1. 28 2. 31 3. 7 4. 5 5. 12 6. 25
7. 3 8. 12 9. 12 10. 12 11. 10 12. 3 13. 36 14. 2
15. 6 16. 23 17. 60 18. 2 19. 12 20. 8 21. yes

Worksheet 61 O. 45% A. 125% A. 1.4% A. $12\frac{1}{2}$
R. 60 R. 4.5 W. .045 A. 0.06 E. 0.12 C. 0.60
P. $\frac{45}{100}$ O. $\frac{72}{100}$ D. 91:100 G. 9:100 B. 400:100
"THERE NEVER WAS A GOOD WAR OR A BAD
PEACE"

Worksheet 62 1. c 2. b 3. b 4. 3% 5. $14\frac{1}{2}$%
6. $25\frac{3}{4}$% 7. $18\frac{1}{3}$% 8. 5 9. $56\frac{1}{2}$ 10. 100 11. $\frac{1}{4}$
12. 23%, 0.23, $\frac{23}{100}$ 13. 89%, 0.89, $\frac{89}{100}$

Worksheet 63 2. 0.08 3. 0.24 4. 0.92
5. 0.5 6. 0.8 7. 1.49 8. 1.08 9. 1.5 10. 1.8
11. 8.0 12. 0.625 13. 0.0625 14. 0.018 15. 0.8075
16. 1.005 17. 0.024 18. 0.0875 19. 2.4 20. 0.725
21. 0.0475 22. 0.005
QUEEN ALEXANDRA BIRDWING

Worksheet 64 1. a 2. c 3. c 4. b 5. a 6. b
7. 0.25 8. 0.17 9. 0.83 10. 0.05 11. 0.02 12. 0.065
13. 2.105 14. 3.08 15. 1.01 16. 0.079 17. 0.823
18. 0.1225 19. 0.015 20. 0.007 21. 0.0075
22. 0.0035 23. 0.0002 24. 0.0085

Worksheet 65 1. c 2. b 3. a 4. b 5. b 6. a
7. 9% 8. 56% 9. 30% 10. 60% 11. 112% 12. 240%
13. 300% 14. 21% 15. 88.25% 16. 151.5%
17. 81.1% 18. 2.51% 19. 25% 20. 72.5% 21. 0.05%
22. 0.625% 23. 210% 24. 450%

Worksheet 66 A. 4% U. 43% E. 79% H. 40%
O. 166% N. 140% U. 180% T. 66% H. 87%
U. 6% H. 10% D. 60% I. 187% G. 203%
A. 10.8% C. 7.9% N. 1.4% T. 68% M. 45%
R. 179% I. 425% N. 400% D. 700% S. 31%
N. 9% T. 0.4% A. 0.79%
THE DIAMOND SUTRA: TUN-HUANG, CHINA

Worksheet 67 1. a. 102% b. 104% c. 105%
d. 107% e. 103% f. 109% g. 108% h. 106%
2. a. 109% b. 111% c. 108% d. 106% 3. a. 38%
b. 138%

Worksheet 68 1. b 2. c 3. a 4. c 5. a 6. $\frac{9}{20}$
7. $\frac{7}{25}$ 8. $\frac{1}{5}$ 9. $\frac{1}{6}$ 10. $\frac{81}{200}$ 11. $\frac{3}{16}$ 12. $\frac{5}{8}$ 13. $\frac{1}{9}$
14. $\frac{1}{11}$ 15. $\frac{7}{100}$ 16. $\frac{7}{50}$ 17. $\frac{1}{200}$ 18. $1\frac{13}{20}$ 19. $2\frac{1}{8}$
20. $3\frac{1}{3}$ 21. $\frac{9}{20}$ 22. $\frac{7}{8}$ 23. $\frac{11}{12}$ 24. $4\frac{4}{5}$ 25. $2\frac{9}{100}$
26. $\frac{15}{16}$

Worksheet 69 2. $\frac{1}{6}$ 3. $\frac{3}{25}$ 4. $\frac{1}{5}$ 5. $\frac{3}{8}$ 6. $\frac{7}{20}$
7. $1\frac{1}{5}$ 8. $\frac{1}{2}$ 9. $\frac{5}{6}$ 10. $\frac{2}{25}$ 11. $1\frac{1}{10}$ 12. $\frac{1}{8}$ 13. $\frac{1}{20}$
14. $3\frac{9}{25}$ 15. $\frac{9}{10}$ 16. $\frac{1}{16}$ 17. $\frac{7}{10}$ 18. $\frac{5}{3}$ 19. $\frac{3}{4}$
20. $\frac{5}{16}$ 21. $\frac{3}{20}$ 22. $\frac{9}{20}$ 23. $\frac{5}{8}$ 24. $\frac{7}{8}$ 25. $\frac{7}{25}$
ELIZABETH STANTON SENECA FALLS

Worksheet 70 1. $\frac{1}{4}$ 2. $\frac{1}{2}$ 3. $\frac{3}{4}$ 4. $\frac{1}{10}$ 5. $\frac{1}{3}$ 6. $\frac{2}{5}$
7. $\frac{2}{3}$ 8. $\frac{4}{5}$ 9. $1\frac{1}{2}$ 10. $1\frac{1}{5}$ 11. $1\frac{1}{4}$ 12. 2 13. HAPPY
BIRTHDAY TO YOU

Worksheet 71 1. c 2. a 3. b 4. a 5. 30%
6. 20% 7. 75% 8. $87\frac{1}{2}$% 9. $56\frac{1}{4}$% 10. 76%
11. $37\frac{1}{2}$% 12. 100% 13. $41\frac{2}{3}$% 14. $63\frac{7}{11}$%
15. 170% 16. 640%

Worksheet 72 2. $62\frac{1}{2}$% 3. $66\frac{2}{3}$% 4. 83%
5. 55% 6. 32% 7. 20% 8. $83\frac{1}{3}$% 9. 40% 10. 16%
11. $36\frac{4}{11}$% 12. 100% 13. 120% 14. $162\frac{1}{2}$%
15. 125% 16. 160% 17. 175% 18. $111\frac{1}{9}$% 19. 6%
20. 320% 21. 550% 22. 10% 23. 22%
AFL

Worksheet 73 1. b 2. a 3. c 4. a 5. 36.08
6. 9.35 7. 0.072 8. 84 9. 105 10. 40.32 11. 96.32
12. 26.7 13. 0.75 14. 105.35 15. 0.072 16. 8,730
17. 32 18. 0.0576 19. 80 20. 0.455 21. 360
22. 30.96

Worksheet 74 1. a 2. b 3. a 4. a 5. c 6. c 7. b
8. 70% 9. 200% 10. 300% 11. 50% 12. 250%
13. 40%

Worksheet 75 1. b; c 2. b; c 3. c; b 4. b; a 5. b;
c 6. b; c

Worksheet 76 1. 75% 2. 20% 3. 100% 4. 60%
5. 40% 6. 25% 7. 10% 8. 20% 9. $33\frac{1}{3}$% 10. $12\frac{1}{2}$%
11. 25% 12. 150% 13. 30% 14. 75% 15. 100%
16. 60% 17. $37\frac{1}{2}$% 18. 90% 19. 20% 20. 1.2%
21. $66\frac{2}{3}$% 22. 70% 23. 35% 24. $12\frac{1}{2}$% 25. 25%
26. $66\frac{2}{3}$% 27. 22.6% 28. 500%

Worksheet 77 1. $0.01 \times n = 68$; 6,800
2. $0.02 \times 6,250 = n$; 125 3. $3,000 = n \times 75,000$; 4%
4. $98 = 0.05 \times n$; 1,960 5. $0.1 \times n = 62$; 620
6. $160 = n \times 800$; 20% 7. $n = 0.25 \times 21.6$; 5.4
8. $69 = n \times 92$; 75% 9. $0.4 \times 375 = n$; 150
10. $800 = n \times 320$; 250% 11. $1.25\% = 72 \times n$; 90
12. $n \times 316.5 = 37.98$; 12%

Worksheet 78 2. 200 3. 7 4. 90 5. 96 6. 51
7. 96 8. 27 9. 20 10. 27 11. 55 12. 27 13. 28
14. 45 15. 500 16. 400 17. 55 18. 250 19. 28
"NOT WITH A BANG BUT A WHIMPER"

Worksheet 79 1. 48 2. 33 3. $9.60 4. 54
5. 81 6. $1.80 7. 84 8. 8 9. 99 10. 20% 11. 50%
12. 10% 13. 25% 14. 25 15. 60 16. 300 17. 1,600
18. 30 19. 40 20. 7 21. 15 22. 120

Worksheet 80 1. yes 2. no 3. yes 4. yes 5. no
6. no 7. 10×5; 50; $\frac{50}{2}$; 25 8. $3 \times n$; $3n$; $\frac{3n}{3}$; 16
9. 5×12; 60; $\frac{60}{3}$; 20 10. $9 \times n$; $9n$; $\frac{9n}{9}$; 4

Worksheet 81 1. c 2. b 3. a 4. b

Worksheet 82 2. 54 3. 76 4. 94 5. 50
6. 12 7. 34 8. 36
ANESTHETIC

Worksheet 83 1. 18 ft 6 in. 2. 14 yd 1 ft 1 in.
3. 7 yd 2 ft 4. 4 yd 2 ft 10 in. 5. 20 yd 6. 15 yd 4 in.
7. 5 yd 1 ft 9 in. 8. 6 yd 1 ft 8 in.

Worksheet 84   **1.** 72 **2.** 7; 252 **3.** 5; 69 **4.** 12
5. 2; 75 **6.** 7; 25 **7.** 6; 8 **8.** 12 **9.** 3; 8
CHILE

Worksheet 85   **2.** 124 **3.** 14,560 **4.** 35,800 **5.** 19
6. 249 **7.** 158 **8.** 360 **9.** $\frac{5}{8}$ **10.** $\frac{17}{20}$ **11.** $\frac{3}{16}$ **12.** $\frac{3}{4}$
PAN

Worksheet 86   **1.** divide; 32 **2.** multiply; 128
3. divide; 2 **4.** multiply; 16 **5.** 7 gal 1 qt
6. 11 qt 1 pt 8 oz **7.** 2 pt 8 oz **8.** 3 gal 2 qt
9. 13 gal 2 qt **10.** 2 qt 11 oz **11.** 2 qt 6 oz
12. 3 gal 2 qt 11 oz

Worksheet 87   **A.** 120 **B.** 56 **A.** 416 **I.** 71 **E.** 17
A. 160 **C.** 8 **I.** 5 **R.** 45 **S.** 35 **E.** 26 **T.** 7 **H.** 54
S. 23 **P.** 6 **G.** $\frac{1}{8}$ **R.** $\frac{3}{8}$ **M.** $\frac{5}{8}$ **E.** 16 qt **L.** 14 qt
F. 34 qt **S.** 11qt
LAMBERT-FISHER ICE PASSAGE

Worksheet 88   **1.** 366 **2.** 1,826 **3.** 7 **4.** 210 **5.** 15
6. 3,287 **7.** 56 **8.** 15 **9.** 18 **10.** 21 h 2 min **11.** 39 s
12. 74 yr 3 mo **13.** 1 wk 3 da

Worksheet 89   **2.** 18 **3.** 233 **4.** 39 **5.** 160
6. 546 **7.** 19 **8.** $\frac{5}{12}$ **9.** $\frac{1}{3}$ **10.** $\frac{1}{6}$ **11.** $\frac{3}{5}$ **12.** 226
"THE WORK OF THE INDIVIDUAL STILL REMAINS
THE SPARK THAT MOVES MANKIND AHEAD."

Worksheet 90   **1.** b **2.** a **3.** 14.4 m **4.** $9\frac{1}{8}$
5. 14 ft 6 in. **6.** 200 cm **7.** 392 yd

Worksheet 91   **2.** 10.18 km **3.** 368 mm **4.** 287 m
5. $14\frac{1}{8}$ in. **6.** 398 mm **7.** $318 **8.** 28 ft **9.** 21 m
A TENNIS COURT

Worksheet 92   **L.** 300 m^2 **O.** 133 ft^2 **D.** 34.6 cm^2
I. 687 mm^2 **A.** 312 km^2 **E.** 1.65 yd^2 **K.** 665 cm^2
N. 38.7 in.^{2} **L.** 633 ft^2 **O.** 365 ft^2 **N.** 333 ft^2
H. 100 yd^2 **L.** 6.46 cm^2 **O.** 0.112 km^2 **I.** 612 in.^{2}
V. 146 m^2 **R.** 1.87 cm^2 **E.** 697 yd^2
HOOVER LANDON WILLKIE

Worksheet 93   **1.** b **2.** a **3.** c **4.** b **5.** c **6.** 169 m^2
7. 6.25 cm^2 **8.** 16 yd^2 **9.** 158.76 mm^2 **10.** $32\frac{1}{9}$ ft^2
11. $56\frac{1}{4}$ in.^{2} **12.** 196 m^2 **13.** 1 mi^2

Worksheet 94   **2.** 56 in. **3.** 247 m **4.** 82.5 mm
5. 20 yd **6.** 51.64 km **7.** 763 ft **8.** 153.86 m
9. 439.6 yd **10.** 204.1 mi **11.** 39.5 cm **12.** 210 m
13. 87.4 ft **14.** 170 m **15.** 29.5 cm **16.** 468 mm
CHARLES IVES

Worksheet 95   **1.** c **2.** b **3.** 19.625 ft^2
4. 2,122.64 cm^2 **5.** 13.8474 m^2 **6.** 0.2826 mm^2
7. 2,920.985 in.^{2} **8.** 0.1256 mi^2 **9.** 615.44 ft^2

Worksheet 96   **1.** multiply; 9 **2.** divide; 640 **3.** c
4. b **5.** b **6.** a **7.** 1,152 **8.** 2,592 **9.** 3,072 **10.** 675
11. 3.25 **12.** 9 **13.** $\frac{1}{2}$ **14.** $\frac{1}{3}$

Worksheet 97   **1.** divide; 27 **2.** multiply; 1,728
3. multiply; 46,656 **4.** divide; 1,728 **5.** 266.8
6. 6,220.8 **7.** $\frac{1}{2}$ **8.** 1.5 **9.** $6\frac{1}{3}$ **10.** 3.4
11. 233,280 **12.** 97,977.6 **13.** $\frac{1}{6}$ **14.** $\frac{8}{9}$

Worksheet 98   **1.** 864 in.^{2} **2.** 576 in.^{2} **3.** 288 in.^{2}
4. 1,152 in.^{2} **5.** 345.6 in.^{2} **6.** 172.8 in.^{2} **7.** 18 ft^2

Worksheet 99   **1.** 46 g **2.** 500 g **3.** 7.5 kg
4. 2 kg **5.** 1 mg **6.** 4 L **7.** 250 mL **8.** 400 L
9. 15 mL **10.** 6 km **11.** centimeters **12.** millimeter
13. millimeters **14.** centimeters **15.** kilometers
16. millimeters **17.** meters **18.** meters **19.** kilometers
20. centimeters

Worksheet 100   1. 6,000   2. 5   3. $\frac{1}{4}$ 4. 96,000   5. 2
6. 3,520   7. $4\frac{1}{4}$ 8. $\frac{1}{2}$ 9. 24   10. $\frac{5}{6}$ 11. 16   12. 7
13. 26   14. 13   15. 29 ft   16. 70 lb 8 oz   17. 4 gal 3 qt
18. 3 yd 2 ft   19. 18 qt   20. 14 lb   21. 3 lb 12 oz
22. 1 T 300 lb   23. 3 lb 5 oz   24. 26 h 20 min   25. 21 h
26. 21 h 9 min   27. 33lb; 11 lb   28. $1.47

Worksheet 101   1. 383.916 g   2. 194.453 kg
3. 1,187.421 km   4. 356.2 L   5. 762,361.59 m
6. 290.76 g   7. 48.4468 m   8. 545.49 cm
9. 175.732 mL   10. 6.98144 mg   11. 0.8526 cm
12. 29.38 L   13. 6,150 mg   14. 8.168 g   15. 72.18 mL
16. 23.14 mm   17. 15.925 g   18. 61.6087 g

Worksheet 102   1. 4 symbols   2. $1\frac{1}{2}$ symbols
3. $7\frac{1}{2}$ symbols   4. $1\frac{1}{4}$ symbols   5. 8 million   6. 5 million
7. $8\frac{1}{2}$ million   8. $9\frac{1}{2}$ million   9. Pictographs may vary
slightly.

Worksheet 103   1. c   2. b

Worksheet 104   1. b   2. b

Worksheet 105   2. 4   3. 5.5   4. 4.5   5. July   6. Jan
7. June   8. May   9. Aug   10. 3.5   11. 2.5   12. 6.5
13. 2.5   14. 3.5   15. 8.5   16. 2   17. 7   18. 8
CELT

Worksheet 106   O. 60   E. 90   L. 40   B. 25   P. 55
R. 50   J. 15   N. 30   U. MN   Z. WY   I. TN   T. UH
BENITO PABLO JUAREZ

Worksheet 107   A. 20%   I. 25%   L. $7\frac{1}{2}$%   E. $\frac{1}{5}$
W. $\frac{1}{4}$ E. $\frac{3}{10}$ R. $\frac{1}{20}$ U. $\frac{1}{8}$ H. $\frac{3}{40}$ N. 45   G. 34
A. 18   T. 28
AMELIA EARHART, LAST SEEN IN NEW GUINEA

Worksheet 108   Answers may vary. 1. circle   2. line
3. bar   4. bar   5. circle   6. line   7. bar

Worksheet 109   1. 30%; 108°   2. 45%; 162°   3. 12%;
43°   4. 6%: 22°   5. 7%: 25°   6. $1.00: 100%: 360°

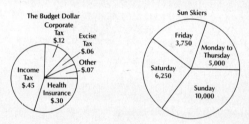

Worksheet 110   2. 53   3. 74   4. 72   5. 58   6. 34
7. 73   8. 54   9. 13   10. 18
GIOVANNI DA VERRAZANO

Worksheet 111   Coordination: 11; 7; 14; 4; 19
Endurance: 7; 3; 10; 2; 15

Worksheet 112   1. −10   2. $\frac{1}{2}$ 3. 28   4. −45
5. −6.75   6. 7.005   7. 107   8. $-\frac{3}{21}$ 9. −1,250
10. $50\frac{1}{4}$ 11. $-\frac{7}{2}$ 12. 20.45   13. 10   14. 6   15. $\frac{1}{2}$
16. 8.3   17. 54   18. $\frac{7}{9}$ 19. 0.081   20. $4\frac{4}{5}$ 21. 4.06
22. 1.91   23. 87.4   24. 3,268   25. 2,3,4,5,6,7,8,9,10
26. −8, −7, −6, −5, −4, −3, −2, −1   27. −4, −3, −2, −1, 0,
1, 2, 3, 4

Worksheet 113   2. −3   3. $\frac{5}{8}$ 4. 0.42   5. $-\frac{1}{3}$ 6. −0.7
7. 14   8. 5.45   9. $-\frac{2}{9}$ 10. $-3\frac{3}{7}$ 11. 0.005   12. 6.006
13. $-2\frac{1}{10}$ 14. $\frac{8}{5}$ 15. 15   16. 0.025   17. $6\frac{2}{3}$ 18. 141.3
19. $\frac{13}{484}$
EGO

Answers

Worksheet 114   1. G 2. C 3. E 4. H 5. J 6. A

7. K 8. B

9.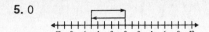

10.

11.

12. −4, 0, 6   13. −7, −1, 3, 7   14. −7, −5, −3, 0, 6

Worksheet 115   1. > 2. > 3. < 4. < 5. 12 6. 32

7. 4 8. 0 9. −2 10. 8 11. 0 12. 3 13. −8 14. −11

15. −3 16. 4 17. 0 18. −5 19. −11 20. −9 21. true

22. true 23. false 24. false 25. false 26. false

27. true 28. false 29. true

Worksheet 116   1. < 2. > 3. > 4. < 5. > 6. >

7. $\frac{1}{12}$, $\frac{1}{8}$, $\frac{1}{4}$, $\frac{1}{3}$, $\frac{3}{8}$, $\frac{5}{12}$, $\frac{7}{12}$, $\frac{2}{3}$, $\frac{3}{4}$, $\frac{5}{6}$ 8. $-1\frac{5}{6}$, $-1\frac{3}{4}$,

$-1\frac{2}{3}$, $-1\frac{1}{2}$, $-1\frac{5}{12}$, $-1\frac{1}{3}$ 9. $13\frac{1}{2}$ ft above, $13\frac{1}{3}$ ft above,

$12\frac{5}{6}$ ft above, $12\frac{1}{2}$ ft above, $12\frac{1}{3}$ ft below, $12\frac{3}{4}$ ft below,

$15\frac{1}{4}$ ft below, $15\frac{1}{3}$ ft below

Worksheet 117

1. −4

2. −9

3. 4

4. −4

5. 0

6. −14 7. 15 8. −7 9. 4 10. −8 11. −12 12. 2

13. −15 14. 27 15. −29 16. −3 17. 0

Worksheet 118

1. 4

2. 5

3. 1.5

4. 3

5. 100 6. −23.5 7. $-\frac{2}{3}$ 8. $\frac{1}{2}$ 9. 0.23 10. 5.346

11. g 12. d 13. b 14. f 15. c

Worksheet 119

1. 3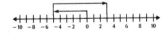

2. 7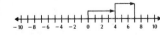

3. −10

4. 5

5. −10

6. −6 **7.** 6 **8.** −12 **9.** 10 **10.** −13 **11.** −5.5 **12.** −3.2
13. 14 **14.** $-3\frac{1}{2}$

Worksheet 120 **2.** 76 **3.** 20 **4.** −38 **5.** −45 **6.** 38
7. 94.1 **8.** −19 **9.** −37 **10.** −35.4 **11.** 6.8 **12.** 47.1
13. −29.8 **14.** −17 **15.** 20 **16.** 59 **17.** −40
RICHARD HENRY DANA

Worksheet 121 **1.** + **2.** + **3.** − **4.** + **5.** + **6.** −
7. + **8.** + **9.** − **10.** −30 **11.** 56 **12.** 54 **13.** 50
14. −72 **15.** −132 **16.** 150 **17.** −42 **18.** 54 **19.** −45
20. −72 **21.** 49 **22.** −48 **23.** −60 **24.** 15 **25.** 10
26. 50 **27.** 2 **28.** 0 **29.** −3

Worksheet 122 **1.** − **2.** + **3.** − **4.** + **5.** + **6.** −
7. 2 **8.** −3 **9.** 16 **10.** 21 **11.** −1.2 **12.** 40 **13.** 0
14. −80 **15.** −9 **16.** 7 **17.** 12 **18.** −9 **19.** −13
20. −4 **21.** −6 **22.** −70 **23.** 17 **24.** −8 **25.** −12
26. −3.6 **27.** 7 **28.** −32 **29.** 27 **30.** 4

Worksheet 123 **1.** −0.09 **2.** $-\frac{3}{5}$ **3.** −213.27 **4.** $7\frac{2}{3}$
5. true **6.** false **7.** false **8.** true **9.** false **10.** false
11. 3.5 **12.** −37.3 **13.** $-\frac{9}{7}$ **14.** 9 **15.** $\frac{7}{8}$ **16.** −20
17. 80 **18.** −40 **19.** −32 **20.** 24 **21.** 800 **22.** −8,000
23. −8 **24.** 500 **25.** −13 **26.** −11 **27.** −29 **28.** 3
29. −3 **30.** −160 **31.** $-\frac{24}{25}$ **32.** 5 **33.** −32 **34.** −4
35. 25

Worksheet 124 **1.** 3 **2.** −13 **3.** 312.8 **4.** 210
5. −0.392 **6.** 49 **7.** −273 **8.** 2.352 **9.** −265
10. 126.2 **11.** −2.19 **12.** −3.69 **13.** 12 **14.** 144
15. −192 **16.** −72 **17.** 31.5625 **18.** 8.75 min

Worksheet 125 **2.** 10 − 6 **3.** $\sqrt{m}$ **4.** $3m$ **5.** xy
6. 5 + k **7.** m^2 **8.** 5 − k **9.** $b^2 + h$ **10.** $\frac{1}{5}(g + k)$
11. $\frac{5}{g+k}$ **12.** 5(g + k) **13.** $\frac{x}{y}$
"ALL THE WORLD'S A STAGE AND ALL THE MEN AND
WOMEN MERELY PLAYERS..."

Worksheet 126 **1.** b **2.** a **3.** a **4.** b **5.** 6 **6.** 36
7. 74 **8.** 4 **9.** 245 **10.** 525 **11.** $1\frac{1}{2}$ **12.** 15 **13.** 7
14. 66 **15.** 10 **16.** 96 **17.** 24 **18.** 80 **19.** 6

Worksheet 127 R. 481 R. 362 I. 484 S. 366
H. 364 S. 485 A. 482 T. 363 A. 480 O. 365
O. 361 M. 483
PORTHOS ARAMIS

Worksheet 128 **2.** $2n - 5 = 8$ **3.** $5 + n \neq 5$
4. $2x + 3 \leq 6$ **5.** $5 - n \geq 5$ **6.** $5n \not> 15$
7. $\frac{x}{4} \not< 9$ **8.** $2n + 8 > 5$ **9.** $\frac{x}{4} = 9$
10. $2x - 3 \geq 6$ **11.** $4 < x < 9$ **12.** $\frac{5n}{8} < 1$
THE LIBERTY BELL

Worksheet 129 **1.** b **2.** a **3.** c **4.** b **5.** c **6.** c
7. a **8.** divide by 7; $a = 8$ **9.** subtract 12; $c = 8$

Worksheet 130 **2.** 30 **3.** 56 **4.** 46 **5.** 28 **6.** 58
7. 32 **8.** 50 **9.** 54 **10.** 14 **11.** 24 **12.** 18 **13.** 52
14. 10 **15.** 12 **16.** 20 **17.** 42 **18.** 36 **19.** 48
"A GOVERNMENT OF LAWS AND NOT OF MEN"

Worksheet 131 **1.** a **2.** c **3.** Add $3.68 to both sides
of the equation. **4.** Add 30 to both sides of the equation.
5. $n = 2$ **6.** $a = 51.9$ **7.** $c = -5$ **8.** $a = 0$
9. $a = 15$ **10.** $y = -4.6$ **11.** $d = 7\frac{3}{5}$ **12.** $x = 26$

Answers

Worksheet 132   L. 11   L. 9   A. 5   R. 19   H. 33
V. –14   E. 0   M. $1\frac{7}{8}$ M. 41   I. 7.7   E. –57   N. $3\frac{1}{8}$
L. 8.8

HERMAN MELVILLE

Worksheet 133   1. c   2. b   3. Subtract 12.3 from both
sides of the equation. 4. Subtract $2\frac{1}{2}$ from both sides of
the equation. 5. $a = 16$ 6. $w = 1.4$ 7. $r = 7$
8. $x = 0$ 9. $a = 9$ 10. $b = 7\frac{9}{10}$ 11. $y = 0.45$
12. $b = 23$

Worksheet 134   N. 52   S. 85   T. 21   V. 55   T. 28
R. 59   I. 81   A. 51   U. 22   E. 58   D. 84   R. 89   N. 82
O. 54   H. 50   O. 88   R. 25   W. 80   S. 20

STUART HANOVER WINDSOR

Worksheet 135   E. 5   I. 8   G. 9   E. 11   U. 0   A. $\frac{3}{5}$
S. 28   N. 1   I. 1.5   I. 7   H. –3   D. 0.16   B. –9   N. 12
D. –24   T. –1   H. $\frac{4}{5}$ S. 60   T. 6   B. –5   I. $\frac{7}{22}$ I. –2.5
G. 15   H. –2

HIGHEST INHABITED BUILDINGS IN THE WORLD

Worksheet 136   2. 26   3. 16   4. 28   5. 90
6. 17   7. 40   8. 30   9. 68   10. 96   11. 29   12. 235
NUTS

Worksheet 137   1. $n + 2 < 10; n < 8$
2. $n - 5 > 8; n > 13$ 3. $-3n > 30; n < -10$
4. $\frac{3}{4}n < -6; n < -8$ 5. $-3 + 4n > 5; n > 2$
6. $-2 + \frac{1}{2}n < 4; n < 12$ 7. $-5n \geq 30; n \leq -6$
8. $3n + 10 \leq 16; n \leq 2$ 9. $n - 3 \leq 21; n \leq 24$
10. $\frac{1}{3}n - 10 \neq 2; n \neq 36$

Worksheet 138   1. 33   2. 8   3. 3   4. 53   5. 45
6. 12   7. 12   8. 3   9. –15   10. 4   11. 42   12. 52
13. 48   14. –12   15. 20   16. 16   17. $\frac{1}{3}$ 18. –20
19. 7   20. $\frac{7}{40}$ 21. $\frac{5}{12}$ 22. 7   23. 19   24. 4

25. $x < 1$
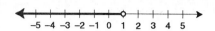

26. $x > 4$

27. $p > 3$

28. $x \geq -4$

Worksheet 139   1. 86.16   2. 921.4   3. 181,650.9
4. 3,374.4   5. 310,223.19   6. 600   7. 2,712.8812
8. 0.625   9. 55.86   10. 412.189   11. –1.85767
12. 282.666   13. 1.4585501   14. –911.08   15. 7
16. 15.9   17. 6.55   18. 176   19. 6.02   20. 147
21. 79   22. 2   23. 4,455.1 mi   24. 82.6 mi/h
25. $b > 8,500$ 26. $x - 328$ 27. 82

Worksheet 140   1. b   2. a   3. c   4. a   5. c   6. (0,6)
7. (1,3)   8. (–3,–4)   9. (3,0)   10. (0,–1)   11. (–2,–1)
12. (6,–2)   13. (–4,3)   14. (–4,0)   15. (4,–6)   16. (6,4)
17. (–6,2)

Worksheet 141   2. R   3. H   4. S   5. I   6. A   7. E
8. T   9. M   10. A   11. D   12. N   13. I   14. G   15. T
16. R   17. D   18. D   19. U   20. S   21. C
MARTHA DANDRIDGE CUSTIS

Worksheet 142

1.–4.

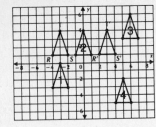

5. (1,0)
6. (5,0)
7. (3,4)
8. (1,2)

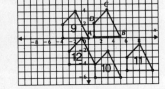

Worksheet 143   **1.** 0; 1; 2 **2.** 0; –2; –4 **3.** –4; –4; –4

4.

5.

6.

Worksheet 144   **1.** 0; 2; –4 **2.** 3; 1; 4 **3.** 0; –2; 4

4. 1; –2; –4 **5.** 2; –1; –4 **6.** 3; 1; 4 **7.** 0; –2; –1

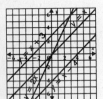

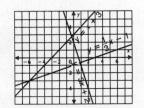

Worksheet 145   **2.** D **3.** L **4.** A **5.** O **6.** N **7.** N

8. D **9.** G **10.** W **11.** N **12.** A

GONDWANALAND

Worksheet 146   **1.** (3,–1) **2.** (–2,4) **3.** (3,0)

4. (0,–4) **5.** (5,2) **6.** (0,6) **7.** (2,–3) **8.** (–5,–3)

9.–16. Check students' graphs.

17.–20.

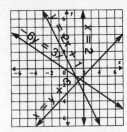

Answers